THE FLANNEL BOARD STORYBOOK

by

FRANCES S. TAYLOR

and

GLORIA G. VAUGHN

Illustrations

LAURIE J. MORRIS

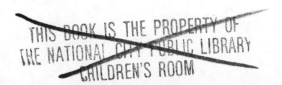

THIS BOOK IS DEDICATED
TO OUR CHILDREN

Cover illustration by Mauro Magellan
Design by Sarah Gregory
Production assistance by Anna Bloomfield

Printed in the United States of America

Library of Congress Cataloging-in-Publication Data

Taylor, Frances S., 1929–
    The flannel board storybook.

 Bibliography: p. 219
    1. Storytelling. 2. Flannelgraphs. 3. Teaching—
Aids and devices. I. Vaughn, Gloria G., 1939–
II. Title.
Z718.3.T38   1986   372.6'4   86-15236
ISBN 0-89334-093-6

Humanics Limited
A Gary B. Wilson Company
P.O. Box 7447
Atlanta, Georgia 30309
(404) 874-2176

CONTENTS

E. HOLIDAY STORIES

THE FLANNEL BOARD STORYBOOK

INTRODUCTION

When we tell a story to a child we are:

- giving a moment of joy
- presenting an exercise in moral development
- sharing an art form
- providing a vehicle for language development
- opening the world of literature
- stimulating the desire to learn to read
- enhancing the ability to fantasize
- imparting the value system of the culture
- providing an antidote to the plastic values of contemporary culture
- sharing a gift of love.

If storytelling is to be a gift of love, it is important to have an understanding of the developmental characteristics of young children and the kind of stories they like and understand.

INFANTS

The infant is totally self-centered. Little exists outside his need for food and nurturance from a caregiver. Ericson defines the developmental task of this first year as the development of trust. An infant must have someone who will respond in a manner that will make him feel that his world is a good, safe place. It is of utmost importance that the infant have his needs met, that he feels valued, and that he has some control over his environment. All the experiences the infant has modify, reflect, and reinforce his sense of trust or lack of trust.

During this first year, the infant forms an attachment to a primary caregiver, usually his mother, and experiences anxiety when separated from that person. These separations are painful at first, but as the infant begins to experience this reality of life and develops a sense of trust, that is that the mother will always return, he can then begin to sense his identity separate from his primary caregiver.

At this stage of development, the infant responds to facial expressions, gestures, postural movements, vocalizations and words. Moms, dads, and other significant caregivers have found that rhythmic repetitions of sound are soothing to babies. These vocalizations help infants to feel secure, thus helping to develop a sense of trust.

Babies enjoy the rhythms of nursery rhymes long before they understand the words. When the baby becomes more attentive to his environment he will enjoy "Pat-a-Cake," "This Little Pig," and fingerplays that relate directly to his own life experiences, particularly those related to his body.

TODDLERS

By the time a child is a year old, he probably understands and says a few significant words and exhibits great joy in imitating sounds he hears. This signals the beginning of a major developmental step. Ericson calls this step "growth toward autonomy." All human beings must develop a separated sense of self and this usually begins during the second year and continues through childhood and into adolescence when it is normally resolved. Some have called two-year-olds the "terrible twos," for as infants begin to establish a sense of self, they have to reject the authority of the parent and other primary caregivers.

During the second year of life a child continues to enjoy the same story forms that were enjoyed as a infant. As language ability increases, the child enjoys stories about the familiar, such as toys, routines, family, and pets. The stories must be brief. The toddler particularly enjoys stories in which his name is used, a reflection of his self-centeredness. Nursery rhymes are greatly enjoyed, especially when repeated with a favorite adult. Encounters with the familiar are reassurng to the toddler. The toddler enjoys repetition of the same stories and repetition within stories.

It is important for parents and caregivers to tell toddlers "when you were a baby" stories. These stories help reassure toddlers that they are mastering life and growing in ability. A "when you were a baby" story might be: "Amy, when you were a baby you drank your milk from a bottle, but now, just look at you, you drink your milk from a glass just like mommy."

You might want to write these stories and draw or paste pictures and write her name and age on the page to be shared time and again with the child.

At this stage of development, a one-to-one relationship with the storyteller is important because of the child's brief attention span and social immaturity. Cuddling, eye contact, and vocalizations reinforce the toddler's development of a sense of trust.

THREES

Young children do not have the ability to form internal images. The young child uses all his senses as he interacts with concrete objects. To truly know something, it must be experienced by the pre-schooler's whole body. Watch a young child with a new toy. He will hold it in his hands, put it in his mouth, rub it over his body, smell it and put it to his ears. The three-year-old becomes truly absorbed in reacting to and with the toy.

Language begins to increase rapidly as the child enters his third year. Threes take great joy in words. One only has to listen to three-year-olds talk during play to know how sophisticated their language can be. Adults sometimes become upset with three-year-olds because they often tell what adults call "tales" or "untruths." Piaget describes the three-year-old's giving of life to inanimate objects, and motives and independent action to animals, as animistic thought. If one has never tried to convince the resident three-year-old that the closet door is not a living, breathing monster, then one has missed a great deal of frustration and challenge. Sometimes it pays to play the game. A three-year-old was asked how he felt we could make the monster happy and in a typical three-year-old manner, he said the monster needed a night light that looked like a big dog and a glass of water on the table beside the bed. This also made a great "when you were a little boy" story for sharing years later.

The three-year-old begins to enjoy stories about friends and animals, especially those with a lot of repetition in them. The repeating of words and phrases is enjoyable and reassuring.

The three-year-old is still immature socially and has great difficulty listening to stories in a group. Words alone are not enough. He must have, at least, clear simple pictures: however, dolls, stuffed toys, puppets and flannel board figures are better choices to help him interiorize. More of his senses are touched with these aids. The child is somewhat rigid now and may demand a story as a ritual. The story before naptime or bedtime helps to ease his fear of the unfamiliar.

FOURS

As the child enters his fourth year of life, he has developed a greater degree of self-control. His language capacity is full and rich and his socialization level is higher. Interest in stories is greater and the ability to sit in a group and listen to a story is possible and enjoyable. The four-year-old, like younger age levels, still enjoys "when you were a baby, one, two, etc." stories that reinforce his sense of mastery especially about fears that have been overcome. Longer stories can be enjoyed because of lengthened attention span.

The four-year-old, like the three-year-old, enjoys stories in which violence is the theme. "The Three Billy Goats Gruff" and "Little Red Riding Hood," told on the parent's or caregiver's lap, help him to safely experience violence and aggression and to work toward overcoming fear. Fantasy is paramount as the child is the pig in the story. The enjoyment of stories where animals act and talk is a reflection of the animistic thought that is characteristic of pre-schoolers.

FIVES

The language capacity of children entering their fifth year has been described as explosive, out of bounds. Fives enjoy new and different words, silly words. This is the age when bathroom language reflects the enjoyment of stories about bodily functions. Fives relate to characters who have tantrums, get dirty, lick their bowls, slurp, cry, snore, growl, whisper, who smell bad and do as they're told not to. They can safely relate to these characters as they reach toward autonomy by rejecting authority. The five-year-old knows he or she is still small and somewhat helpless and enjoys stories where the powerful adult, in animal disguise, doesn't do as told or does something to look ridiculous. Fives are beginning to try to sort out reality from fantasy and will often ask if a story is "real." Fives no longer are the pig in the story. The concrete, the puppet, the doll, or the flannel board figures are still needed to help the five-year-old interiorize. Fives enjoy participation in the story.

SCHOOL-AGERS

The developmental tasks of the young school-age child, according to Ericson, are:

- The development of a sense of initiative, which includes the ability to make plans and carry them out.
- The development of a sense of industry.
- He has the determination to master tasks and thrives on a sense of accomplishment.

Other developmental characteristics of the young school-age child, as they relate to storytelling, are:

- increased language skills
- a dramatically improved memory and lengthened attention span
- a broadened understanding of concepts
- an increased need for self-reliance, independence, and autonomy
- a crystallizing sex role identification
- an increased ability to deal appropriately with anxiety and conflict
- a need for peer acceptance
- the young school-age child sees the world logically and rationally and is now more concerned with the "real", the "true", rather than with fantasy.

These characteristics of the young school-ager tell us that he enjoys longer, more complex stories and our own true stories of when we were children. The school-ager likes to tell his own true story and, with his need for a sense of accomplishment he can, with a group of peers, write plays, design and make sets and costumes and produce traditional plays or puppet plays.

CONCLUSION

Some of the more academic skills which can be developed through story telling are:

- Improved listening skills
- Lengthened attention span
- Increased ability to repeat ideas in sequence
- Expansion of vocabulary
- Understanding of new concepts
- Development of the ability to fantasize and think creatively
- Improvement in the quality of oral language

Stories for the young child:

- must be accompanied by concrete objects to help him interiorize.
- must have interesting subject matter that will help him gradually broaden life's experiences.
- must fit his attention span.
- must fit his social maturity, i.e., from lap stories to sitting in a group sharing a story.
- must help him deal with aggressive feelings and fears in a safe environment.
- must reflect his animistic thought.
- must contribute to an increasing vocabulary and language ability.
- must enrich life and help him toward maturity.

STEP BY STEP DIRECTIONS TO STORYTELLING ON THE FLANNEL BOARD

LEARNING THE STORY

If this is your first attempt at storytelling, you may feel more comfortable if you begin with one of the traditional stories.

If you are learning a new story, these tips will help.

1. First, choose a story that you enjoy. It is hard to "sell" a story you are not enthusiastic about.
2. Read the story.
3. Read it again and picture it like a silent movie.
4. Picture it again without reading it.
5. Read the story aloud. Do not memorize it.
6. Write the story down in your own words.
7. Tell it aloud.

The story will become your own after you have told it three times to an audience. As you become more experienced you will be able to vary details and tailor the story for a particular child or group of children.

YOUR CUSTOM-MADE FLANNEL BOARD

Commercial flannel boards can be purchased; however, it is possible to make a more attractive and functional one with considerably less expense. Two types of flannel boards have been developed especially for the stories in this book.

1. Cover one side of a 4 foot by 2 foot piece of heavy corrugated cardboard (may be the side of a sturdy box) with turquoise felt.
2. Cut a strip of beige felt 4 inches by 48 inches. Scallop one (48") edge of it. Line the straight edge up with the bottom of the board and glue in place to represent the rolling hills in the distance.
3. Cut a strip of green felt 2½ inches by 48 inches. Scallop one (48") edge of it. Line the long straight edge up with the bottom of the board and glue over the beige strip to represent grass.
4. To make the sun, cut a 2-inch circle of red felt for the center. Cut a 4-inch circle of orange felt, then cut it to resemble the sun's rays. Glue the red circle on top of the orange piece and glue the sun in place on the board.
5. Cut 3 or 4 pieces of white felt in the shape of clouds and glue in place.
6. Using the patterns given, houses and trees should be cut from felt. Do not glue them onto the flannel board. They are to be changed and rearranged on the basic flannel board to fit the needs of the particular story you are telling.

DOWN HOME WITH GERALDENE AND OSCAR BEAR

If your children enjoy the bear stories as much as ours have, you may want to make a special flannel board for Geraldene and Oscar Bear's adventures. Follow the first five steps given for the basic flannel board with the additional steps listed below.

1. Make the Bears' House and Grannie's House using the patterns given. Glue the Bears' House to the far left of the board. Glue Grannie's House to the far right.

2. Make the Honey Tree using the pattern and glue it to the left of Grannie's House in the mountains.

3. Make the creek from a strip of blue felt using the pattern and glue it to the left of the mud puddle, which is in the center.

4. Make the enormous mud puddle out of brown felt using the pattern. Glue it to the center of the flannel board. Put sprigs of grass and rocks around its edge.

5. Make several smaller trees from green and brown felt and glue to the background. Sprinkle brightly colored felt flowers on the grass.

MAKING THE FLANNELBOARD FIGURES

We hope to make the job of making the figures in our book as easy as possible. We have used nothing that can't be found at the craft counter in your local discount store, fabric stores, craft centers, and dime stores. The following list contains ideas and suggestions for gathering materials and constructing the flannel board figures.

NON-WOVEN INTERFACING

This is perhaps the easiest way to make the figures. Non-woven interfacing can be purchased from a fabric store. Place the interfacing on top of the pattern, trace it and cut it out. Color the smooth side with crayons or felt tip markers. The rougher side will then stick to the flannel board.

FELT

Cut the figures from felt using the patterns. Additional details can be added with a fine line felt tip pen or by gluing smaller pieces of felt of another color to the figure. This method of construction is most effectively used with patterns having little detail.

LIGHTWEIGHT CARDBOARD

Patterns may be traced with carbon paper onto lightweight cardboard, cut out, and colored with crayons or felt tip markers. Since the cardboard will not stick to the flannel board, it is necessary to glue scraps of felt or coarse sandpaper to the back of the figure. The anti-static foam sheets used in your dyer can be re-cycled and used in place of the felt or sandpaper. Cardboard figures are needed with patterns having more detail.

- FELT purchased by the yard is less expensive than felt squares, and those colors that one uses most often should be purchased by the yard.
- FELT SQUARES (usually 9 X 12 inches in size) should be purchased for unusual colors and small projects.
- TACKY GLUE (a very thick white glue that dries clear) is best for gluing the felt pieces together. Several different brands of this glue are available at craft centers, discount stores, and fabric stores.
- SCISSORS (a good pair of fabric scissors and fingernail scissors) are a must.
- TRIMS, such as lace, rick-rack, eyelet, ribbon, etc., are used to add character and interest to the felt figires. Save leftovers from sewing projects to use with your felt figures.
- PLASTIC WIGGLE EYES (the ones that move when the character moves) add "life" to people and animals. They can be purchased in sizes 3mm to 30mm.

NON-WOVEN INTERFACING can be used to make figures. The slick surfaced, heavy weight kind is easiest to use.

—When making the FELT FIGURES, it is easiest to make a base (called a silhouette) of the figure, to cut pieces of the figure, place them on the silhouette, then glue into place. The solid felt back adheres to the flannel board.

—Remember, when making flannelboards of felt, DO NOT put glue under the felt that covers the flannelboard. The figures are held in place by static electricity, and the airspace between felt and cardboard is where the static electricity is developed. If you have trouble with figures staying on flannelboard, rub entire board with a cloth to charge the static electricity field so the figures will stay in place.

—POM-POMS (small yarn balls) come in a variety of sizes from tiny (the size of a BB) to large (the size of one's fist). They make noses, buttons, tails, etc.

—A HOLE PUNCH can be used to punch circles from felt. The size is perfect for noses, buttons, centers of flowers, etc.

—EMBROIDERY FLOSS (THREAD) can be used for making shoe-laces, bows, whiskers, tails, hair, etc.

—POLYESTER FIBERFILL can be used for clouds, beards, stuffing, etc.

—SEQUINS, BEADS, RHINESTONES can be used to make jewelry and to add glitter to the characters.

—GLITTER adds sparkle, interest, and motion to the figures.

—PLASTIC WRAP or CELLOPHANE can be used to give the idea that houses and vehicles have glass in them.

—FEATHERS and FAKE FUR can be used on the figures to give added interest and character.

—PIPE CLEANERS (CHENILLE STEMS) can be used for support and decoration.

THE STORYTELLER'S APRON

The Storyteller's Apron is a device for gaining and holding the attention of a group of children at Story Time. Do you ask children to put on their listening ears and looking eyes, to sit like Indians and to keep their hands to themselves during Story Time? Do you need to interrupt the story to remind children of the rules? Do you sometimes need to ask a disruptive child to leave the group? Do you have some children who'd rather not come to Story Time?

If you answered yes to any of these questions, you are not alone! Many of us have had problems holding children's interest at Story Time. As a beginning teacher, I worried that if I allowed one bored child to leave the group, my whole audience would leave.

When I took another look at Story Time, I decided that it was up to me to make it so special, so exciting that all the children would want to be there, and to listen to every word of the story. The Storyteller's Apron is the device I developed to do this for me.

A Storyteller's Apron can be one you make especially for that purpose. Mine is a denim chef's apron with brightly colored felt pockets of a variety of sizes and shapes. Any apron you already have will do as well after you add pockets. A long gathered skirt would have even more pockets. One of the pockets will contain a tiny stuffed dog or other animal who is the key to the success of the Storyteller's Apron. He will set the standards for Story Time, freeing you and your children to fully enjoy the story without interruptions. You will put in each of the other pockets a small trinket that ties into the stories you plan to tell. For example, a small plastic pig could introduce "The Three Little Pigs" or an Easter egg might introduce "Mrs. Easter Chicken."

USING THE STORYTELLER'S APRON

After you have put on the apron, gather the children closely around you. Introduce the apron to the children by asking what it is, who they have seen wearing an apron, and what people usually do when wearing an apron. Next, tell them that the apron you are wearing is a special apron, that you're not going to cook or wash dishes because this is a Storyteller's Apron. Point out the pockets, talking about their colors, sizes and shapes. Tell the children that there are stories in the pockets. Next, ask the children if they'd like to meet your little friend who is in the red pocket.

"My little friend is teeny tiny. He's just one year old, not nearly as big as you are. Sometimes he gets scared. Do you ever get scared? Do you like to sit on your mom's lap when you are scared? My little friend likes to sit in my hand when he's scared. He gets scared when people make a lot of noise or when they jump around too much. That's because he is so teeny tiny.

Would you like me to see if I can get him to come out of the pocket? You would? All right, I'll try, but you must be very quiet and very still so he doesn't get scared." (Peek into the pocket, patting it gently with your other hand and whisper): "Oh, he's asleep! Do you want to help me wake him up? You do? Then let's all very softly call him to come out."

(As you softly repeat, "Wake-up," gently pull the dog out, allowing only the head to show above the pocket.)

"Oh, look. He's coming out. Now remember to be very quiet and very still so that he won't get scared. If he gets scared, he'll go back into the pocket."

(Hold the dog in the palm of your hand, patting him gently. Talk about how soft he is. Still holding him, allow the children to take turns patting him, praising them for being so quiet and so gentle with him.)

"The little dog is a Story Dog. That means he is magic. Sometimes he talks to me, not always, though. I have to put him right up to my ear and listen very hard because he has a teeny tiny voice. Let's see if he wants to say anything."

(Put the dog to your ear, pretending to listen, asking him to talk just a little louder so you can hear him.)

"Oh, he said something! He said, 'You are the nicest children he has ever seen.' He liked the way you are so quiet and the way you patted him so gently. He said that after we have a story he'd like to talk to each one of you. Now, he wants me to tell a story. Story Dog loves stories. He said there is a story in the purple pocket that he knows you will like. I'll look in there and see what story it is."

(Reach into the pocket and pull out whatever you have put in the pocket to introduce the story you plan to tell. Encourage the children to talk about it. Pass the object around, allowing each child to hold it. After everyone has seen it, return it to the pocket.)

"Now I'm ready to tell the story. The Story Dog likes this story very much and he wants to hear it, too. I'll put him right here by me so he can hear. Just look how nicely he is sitting. He is being very still and very quiet just like you are."

(After the story is finished, pick up the dog and pretend to listen.) "The Story Dog liked that story. He hopes you did, too. He said you were very good listeners. Would you like to see if he will talk to you now?"

Allow each child to put the dog to his ear, reminding them that he doesn't always talk and that they will need to listen very hard. Children having vivid imaginations will report delightful conversations with the Story Dog. Other children quickly catch on to the fantasy. If a very literal minded child seems puzzled when the dog doesn't talk to him, a warm smile and a reminder that he doesn't always talk will smooth it over. Later on that child will be ready to enter into the make-believe play.

After each child has had a turn to listen to the Story Dog, ask them to tell him good-bye. Put him gently back in the pocket.

Pat the pocket, telling him "Nighty-night." Put the apron away so that it is used only to set the stage for Story Time. I sometimes tell the children that the Story Dog needs to sleep a lot just like little babies do and that he will sleep in the red pocket until it's Story Time again. After a while, the little dog may lose his magic and you may want to introduce a new stuffed animal from time to time.

As you can see, you won't need to repeat the rules for Story Time. The Story Dog reminds children of rules by modeling what is expected of them.

READY, SET, GO!

You know your story. You've made your flannel board and the figures for your story. Your Storyteller's Apron is ready. Forget your butterflies and begin! It's not necessary to give a perfect performance with this story. Your children's enthusiastic reception of your efforts will more than reward you for your hard work and encourage you to prepare more stories.

Storytelling, at its best, is an intensely intimate experience. The impact of the story depends upon the storyteller's ability to transport each child from this setting and the group to the land of make believe. The artful storyteller spins the magic of the story around each child and takes him on a private journey into the realm of fantasy. These are some tips to establish this feeling of intimacy and to intensify the impact of the story.

• Stack the figures in the order in which they are to be introduced. It will add to the suspense if you hide them in a special box or basket until they are placed on the flannel board.

• Find a comfortable, quiet place to tell the story. You might sit on the floor with the children or on a low stool. It is important that you be on the children's eye level and that they be very close to you.

• Place the flannel board against the wall so that it leans slightly backward. This will help to keep the figures in place.

• If this is the first time your children have heard a flannel board story, let them examine the figures and explain to them why they stick to the flannel board before you begin. Otherwise, they may be so interested in the magic of the figures sticking to the flannel board that they may miss the story!

• As you tell the story, look directly into each child's eyes. The intensity of direct eye contact generates a feeling of personal involvement in each child.

• Speak in a hushed voice so that children will need to tune out competing sounds and intensify their listening and concentration, focusing completely on the story.

• From time to time, reach out to individual children, gently touching them to draw them more deeply into the fantasy.

- If a child interrupts, go on with the story as you look directly at that child. If that does not work, put his name in the story (i.e. "and, Jason, the bear went over the mountain.") If neither helps, stop the story and assure the child that you want to hear what he has to say after you tell the story.

- Be dramatic! Make use of pauses to build suspense. Use appropriate voices for the characters in the story. Don't be afraid to growl, slurp or snore.

Once, when I told a story without putting myself in it, four-year-old Richard said disappointedly, "You didn't tell it with your eyes!" SO, "Tell it with your eyes" and enjoy the art of storytelling with your own children.

THE BEAR STORIES

GERALDENE AND THE BEARS

Storyteller: This is a story about bears. There are two bears in this story. This is Geraldene Bear and this is Oscar Bear. The bears lived in a pretty little house out in the woods. The house had a red door and yellow curtains in the window.

Now the bears didn't like the winter time. They hated ice and snow. When it was very cold, the bears went to bed. They covered up with all their blankets, even their heads. They slept a long, long time. Finally spring came. The sun melted the ice and snow and the bears woke up. Oscar Bear got out of bed. He stretched and yawned and said:

Oscar Bear: "Oh, I'm hungry. I'm so hungry I could eat a buffalo!"

Storyteller: Geraldene Bear got out of bed. She stretched and yawned and said:

Geraldene Bear: "Oh, I'm so hungry. I'm so hungry I could eat a kangaroo!"

Storyteller: The bears went in the kitchen to look for something to eat for breakfast. They opened the refrigerator and looked inside, but there was nothing to eat. They opened the stove and looked inside, but there was nothing to eat. They opened the pantry and looked inside, but there was nothing to eat. Oscar Bear stamped his feet and jumped up and down.

Oscar Bear: "I want my breakfast. I want breakfast right now. I'm hungry."

Storyteller: Geraldene Bear said:

Geraldene Bear: "Now, Oscar Bear, you just hush that fussing right now. You just stop all that carrying on. I'll get us some breakfast. I'll go to the creek and catch us a nice big fish for breakfast."

Storyteller: Oscar Bear stopped fussing when she said that. He liked fish. As Geraldene Bear was going out the door to catch the fish, he said:

Oscar Bear: "Wait a minute, Geraldene Bear! I want to tell you something and you listen good. Don't go to the Honey Tree. If you go to the Honey Tree the bees will sting you just like they did the last time you went messing around with their honey."

Storyteller: Geraldene Bear said:

Geraldene Bear: "Why, Oscar, I'm surprised you'd think I'd go back to the Honey Tree. I'm not going to any old Honey Tree. I'm going to catch a fish."

Storyteller: She started walking, going to the creek to catch a fish. Well, Geraldene Bear loved honey better than anything in the whole world. She started thinking about that honey. Yum, yum. She smelled something. Ummm! It smelled good. "Sniff, sniff" Do you know what she smelled? (Pause) Right, she smelled the Honey Tree.

The next thing you know, Geraldene Bear went straight to the Honey Tree. The bees were gone. She reached in the hole in the Honey Tree where the bees kept their honey. She started eating honey as fast as she could. "Slurp, slurp." Bears make a lot of noise when they eat. Of course children don't though.

The bees heard Geraldene Bear slurping their honey and they flew back to the Honey Tree. "Bzzzzzz." Geraldene Bear heard the bees and she ran away as fast as she could. She was afraid of bees because they hurt when they sting. She came to the creek and she jumped in the water to hide from the bees. Splash. She was all covered up with the water except her little nose. Her nose was sticking out of the water!

The bees saw Geraldene Bear jump in the creek and they followed her. Bzzzzzzzz! They stung her right on her nose. She jumped up out of the water and said:

Geraldene Bear: "Oh, oh, oh, my nose! My nose hurts! Those bees stung me on my nose."

Storyteller: Poor Geraldene Bear's nose was stuck way out to here. She thought she'd better hurry and catch the fish and get home before the bees came back. She put her big paws in the water and pulled out a nice big fish. She ran home as fast as she could with the big fish. Oscar Bear took one look at Geraldene Bear's nose and he knew where she'd been.

Oscar Bear: "Geraldene Bear, just look at your nose! I told you not to go to the Honey Tree. You were a bad bear. You went to the Honey Tree and the bees stung you on your nose. Just look at your nose."

Storyteller: Geraldene Bear put her paws on her nose and said:

Geraldene Bear: "Oh, Oscar! Yes, I did go to the Honey Tree. Those bees stung me on my nose. My nose hurts so bad. I won't ever go back to the Honey Tree again. I'm sorry, Oscar."

Storyteller: Oscar Bear felt sorry for her. He put a big, big band-aid on her poor nose to make it stop hurting. Then he cooked the fish and gave Geraldene Bear the biggest piece.

Do you think Geraldene bear will go back to the Honey Tree?

BACK TO THE HONEY TREE

Storyteller: One day at the Bears' house in the woods, Geraldene Bear was all alone because Oscar had gone fishing. She started feeling very hungry. She said:

Geraldene Bear: "I declare, I'm about to starve to death!"

Storyteller: Geraldene went in the kitchen to look for something to eat. She looked in the refrigerator and it was full of Frosty Cola. She said:

Geraldene Bear: "I declare, there's nothing in here but Frosty Cola and I don't want any old Frosty Cola."

Storyteller: Then Geraldene Bear looked in the pantry and it was empty except for a big box of Cocoa Capops.

Geraldene Bear: "I declare, there's nothing in here but Cocoa Capops and I don't want any old Cocoa Capops."

Storyteller: Then Geraldene Bear thought and thought about what she was feeling hungry for.

Geraldene Bear: "Ummmmmmmmmmm! What I really want to eat is honey!"

Storyteller: Now, Oscar had told Geraldene Bear not to go to the Honey Tree. She remembered how the bees had stung her nose the last time she got in their honey, but Geraldene Bear just could not stop thinking about the honey. Finally, she decided that if she ran very fast to the Honey Tree she would be home before Oscar came back. So out the door she went. She ran and ran. She came to an enormous mud puddle.

Geraldene Bear: "Oooh, eeee! I am so tired, but I've got to hurry so Oscar won't know I went to the Honey Tree."

Storyteller: And Geraldene Bear ran through the enormous mud puddle as fast as she could. Squish, squish, squish! At last she came to the Honey Tree. She was so tired that she could hardly climb up the Honey Tree to the hole where the bees kept their honey. She put her ear up to the hole and when she didn't hear any bees she started to eat the honey.

Geraldene Bear: "Slurp, slurp, slurp. Mmmmmmmmmmmm, this is good honey."

Storyteller: Well, Geraldene was smacking her lips and licking her chops when she heard something.

Bees: "Bzzzzzz, Bzzzzzzzz, Bzzzzzzzzz."

Storyteller: Poor old Geraldene was so scared when she heard those bees.

Geraldene Bear: "Help, help, help! The bees are after me!"

Storyteller: Geraldene was so full of honey she could hardly run, but she ran and ran until she came to the enormous mud puddle. She was so tired by then that she fell right into the mud puddle. The bees followed Geraldene to the mud puddle. Bzzzzzzzzzzz. So, Geraldene stood up and started hollering as loud as she could.

Geraldene Bear: "Help! Help! Help! Get away from me! Leave me alone! Please don't sting me!"

Storyteller: Geraldene was all covered with mud and she didn't even look like a bear. Those Bees had never seen anything as terrible looking as Geraldene Bear and they were so scared that they flew back to the Honey Tree to hide. Geraldene Bear ran away as fast as she could. She was so scared of the bees that she never even looked back. She ran and ran until she got back to her little house. She ran inside and shut the door and fell down in a heap on the floor. Oscar Bear was still down at the creek fishing.

Geraldene Bear: "Ooooh, eeee! I won't ever go back to that Honey Tree again."

Do you think Geraldene will go back to the Honey Tree?

LITTLE HEBERT (A-BEAR)

Storyteller: Geraldene Bear and Oscar Bear lived in a pretty little house in the woods. In the wintertime when it was very cold, Geraldene Bear and Oscar Bear slept and slept in their warm little house just like this: "Snore, snore, snore." Bears don't like the cold winter.

Finally springtime came with the sunshine and the flowers. Geraldene Bear and Oscar Bear woke up from their long, long sleep and went outside to see the springtime.

A little ball of brown fur toddled along on his fat little legs right behind Geraldene Bear and Oscar Bear. The bears had a brand new little baby bear. This baby bear's name was Hebert (pronounced a-bear). I guess he was a Louisiana bear because all the bears in Louisiana are named Hebert.

Well, Oscar Bear was hungry like he always was when he woke up from his long winter sleep. He stretched and yawned and he said:

Oscar Bear: "Geraldene Bear, do we have any porridge to eat for breakfast?"

Geraldene Bear: "No, Oscar Bear, we ate up all the porridge. I'll go to the creek and catch a nice big fish for breakfast if you'll watch Little Hebert. But, whatever you do, don't let Little Hebert go over the mountain!"

Storyteller: Oscar Bear promised to watch Little Hebert and Geraldene Bear left to go to the creek to catch the fish for breakfast. Oscar Bear sat down under a tree to watch Little Hebert like he'd promised Geraldene Bear he would.

Oscar Bear: "Hebert, you can play right here in the yard. But! whatever you do, do NOT go over the mountain."

Little Hebert: "Oh, I won't go over the mountain, Papa."

Storyteller: So, Little Hebert started picking flowers in the yard. He had never seen flowers before and he thought they must be the prettiest things in the whole world. Pretty soon, Oscar Bear began to get sleepy. He tried and tried to keep his eyes open so he could watch Little Hebert, but he was SO sleepy. I'm sorry to tell you, but Oscar Bear went sound asleep! "Snore, snore, snore."

A beautiful orange butterfly landed on the flower Little Hebert was about to pick. He tried to catch the butterfly, but it was too quick for him and flew away. Little Hebert ran after the butterfly. The butterfly went faster because it didn't want to be caught by a bear. It flew up the side of the mountain. Little Hebert ran and ran up the side of the mountain on his fat little legs after the butterfly. The butterfly flew over the mountain!

Now Oscar was sound asleep, but he had told Little Hebert NOT to go over the mountain. Well . . . what do you think Little Hebert did? That's right.

"The bear went over the mountain,
The bear went over the mountain,
— The bear went over the mountain,
To see what he could see."

When Little Hebert went over the mountain the beautiful butterfly was nowhere to be seen. But Little Hebert ran along on his fat little legs to see what he could see.

What he saw was a pretty little kitty cat. It was black with a white stripe down its back. This was no ordinary kitty cat. This was a skunk! Do you know what skunks do to bears who scare them? They spray terrible stinky stuff all over them!

Little Hebert: "Here kitty, kitty, kitty."

Storyteller: He reached for the skunk with his paw because he wanted to play. But the skunk didn't want to play. He was afraid of Hebert! What do you suppose he did? Yes! He sprayed that terrible stinky stuff all over Little Hebert!

Poor Little Hebert! He smelled terrible! He held his nose and said:

Little Hebert: "Phewee!"

Storyteller: He ran as fast as his fat little legs would carry him back over the mountain to his own yard. Little Hebert smelled so terrible that the smell woke Oscar Bear up.

Oscar Bear: "Phewee, Hebert, you stink. You smell like a skunk!"

Little Hebert: "I'm sorry, Papa. I just wanted to play with the kitty cat."

Storyteller: Oscar Bear knew right away that Little Hebert had gone over the mountain. He held his nose and said:

Oscar Bear: "Oh, dear! What will Geraldene Bear say when she comes home? She knows skunks live on the other side of the mountain. When she smells Little Hebert she will know I went to sleep and let him go over the mountain and get sprayed by a skunk. Geraldene Bear will be mad at me."

Storyteller: Just then Geraldene Bear came home with the fish. She held her nose.

Geraldene Bear: "Phewee, Hebert, you stink! You smell like a skunk."

Little Hebert: "I'm sorry, Mama. I just wanted to play with the kitty cat."

Storyteller: Oscar Bear looked very sad, holding his nose.

Oscar Bear: "Oh, Geraldene Bear, please don't be mad at me! I went to sleep and let Little Hebert go over the mountain. He got sprayed by a skunk. He smells awful! Phewee! Whatever will we do?"

Storyteller: Geraldene Bear looked at Oscar Bear and shook her head. She looked at Little Hebert and shook her head. Then she held her nose.

Geraldene Bear: "Phewee, Oscar Bear, I do declare! I told you not to let Little Hebert go over the mountain!"

Storyteller: Then Geraldene Bear had an idea. She went in the house and got the blue and silver bottle of Evening in London perfume that Oscar Bear had given her for Christmas. She sprayed the whole bottle of Evening in London perfume on Little Hebert!

He sneezed his little head nearly off. "Achoooo! Achoooo! Achoooo!" But he surely did smell better.

Oscar Bear: "I will never ever let Little Hebert go over the mountain again."

Storyteller: Geraldene Bear gave Oscar Bear and Little Hebert each a great big bear hug.

Do you think Little Hebert will ever go over the mountain again?

THE SQUALLIN' BABY

Storyteller: One morning at the Bears' pretty little house in the woods, Little Hebert woke up and he heard:

Martha Mae: "Wah, wah, wah."

Storyteller: Little Hebert said:

Hebert: "What is that racket? It sounds like a squallin' baby, but we don't have any baby . . . or do we?"

Storyteller: Little Hebert got out of bed and peeped around the door. There sat Geraldene holding a little squallin' baby bear.

Martha Mae: "Wah, wah, wah."

Storyteller: Hebert said:

Hebert: "Who is that little old baby bear?"

Geraldene: "Look, Hebert. Here is your brand new little baby sister. This is Martha Mae. Don't you want to hold her?"

Storyteller: Little Hebert said:

Hebert: "I don't want any little old squallin' baby."

Storyteller: Little Hebert would not hold Martha Mae. He wouldn't even look at her. Martha Mae squalled all day long and half the night.

Martha Mae: "Wah, wah, wah."

Storyteller: When Martha Mae finally went to sleep Geraldene put her in a little tiny bed in Hebert's room and then she and Oscar went to sleep in their room.

Geraldene and Oscar: "Snore, snore, snore."

Storyteller: Martha Mae didn't sleep long. She woke up squallin' again.

Martha Mae: "Wah, wah, wah."

Storyteller: All that commotion woke up Hebert.

Hebert: "Quit that squallin', girl, or I'm gonna tear your ears off."

Storyteller: Martha Mae squalled louder than ever.

Martha Mae: "Wah, wah, wah."

Storyteller: Little Hebert said:

Hebert: "I told you to quit that squallin'. Now I'm gonna give you away. I'm gonna give you to Grannie Bear."

Storyteller: Little Hebert picked up Martha Mae and lit out through the woods to Grannie Bear's house. Grannie Bear said:

Grannie Bear: "Well, I'll vow, Little Hebert. Here you are in the middle of the night with your brand new baby sister and her just a-squallin' her head off. Come on in here, child."

Storyteller: Grannie Bear knew just what to do with Martha Mae. She gave her a little taste of honey in a spoon and rocked her to sleep. Then she made Hebert a honey sandwich and soon he was fast asleep, too.

Back at the Bears' house, Geraldene woke up and tiptoed into Hebert's room to see about her bear babies. Well, Martha Mae and Hebert were nowhere to be seen. Geraldene hollered and hollered.

Geraldene: "Help! Help! Help! Oscar, our bear babies are gone! Come quick!"

Storyteller: Geraldene's racket woke up Oscar and he came running. When he saw the babies were gone he said:

Oscar: "Help! Murder! Police! The babies are gone!"

Storyteller: Geraldene cried and hollered, too. Finally she said,

Geraldene: "Oscar, we can't just stand here hollerin' all night. We have to go look for our babies."

Storyteller: Oscar said:

Oscar: "Maybe they went to the creek."

Storyteller: So Oscar and Geraldene, crying and hollerin', ran to the creek, but the bear babies were not at the creek. So Geraldene said:

Geraldene: "Maybe they went to the Honey Tree."

They went to the Honey Tree, but the bear babies were not at the Honey Tree. They called and called their babies.

Geraldene: "Hebert! Martha Mae Bear! Come back!"

Oscar: "Hebert! Martha Mae Bear! Come back!"

Storyteller: But the bear babies didn't answer. Geraldene cried.

Geraldene: "Oh, my poor little babies! They are lost! I'll never see them again!"

Oscar: "Geraldene, you're crying and hollering so loud I can't even think!"

Storyteller: Then Geraldene got quiet so Oscar could think. He said:

Oscar: "Let's go ask Grannie Bear where our babies could be."

Storyteller: So they did. They ran to Grannie Bear's house, but when they got there, they started crying and hollering again.

Bears: "Oh, our babies are lost! Oh, Grannie Bear, we can't find our babies."

Storyteller: Grannie Bear said:

Grannie Bear: "Shhhhhhhh! Can't you see I've got these babies asleep?"

Storyteller: Geraldene and Oscar were so glad to find their babies finally. They carried them home, still asleep, and put them in their little beds. Then they went to sleep in their own room.

Bears: "Snore, snore, snore."

Storyteller: Little Hebert peeped out from under his covers and said to Martha Mae,

Hebert: "If you start that hollerin' and squallin' again, girl, I'm gonna tear your ears off and give you back to Grannie Bear."

Storyteller: Martha Mae didn't say anything. She didn't even squall because she was sound asleep.

Do you think Hebert will tear Martha Mae's ears off and give her back to Grannie Bear?

THE BEARS' WASHDAY

Storyteller: The sun was shining brightly at the pretty little house in the woods where the bears lived. Hebert and Martha Mae Bear had just finished their porridge. They licked their bowls clean.

Bear Babies: "Slurp, slurp."

Storyteller: Of course children don't lick their bowls, but bears do. Geraldene Bear said:

Geraldene Bear: "Hurry, children. We're all going to the creek this morning."

Storyteller: Hebert and Martha Mae Bear were all smiles because they liked to go to the creek. Geraldene Bear took a big box of Bubble-O and all the bears' dirty clothes so that she could do the washing. Oscar Bear took his fishing pole so that he could catch a fish for lunch. Usually bears catch fish with their big paws, but Oscar Bear was sometimes lazy. He liked to take a little nap and let the fish catch itself on the hook on his fishing pole.

When the bears got to the creek Geraldene Bear said:

Geraldene Bear: "Now, Oscar, you watch the babies. Don't you let them go off. I'm going to wash these dirty clothes."

Storyteller: Geraldene started to work with her Bubble-O, washing away.

Oscar Bear settled down to fish. He watched Hebert and Martha Mae Bear for a little while, but Oscar got very sleepy. Soon he was fast asleep.

Oscar Bear: "Snore, snore, snore."

Storyteller: Hebert and Martha Mae Bear played right beside Oscar for awhile. They found a big stick to throw in the creek. It went "kersplash!" It started to float away down the creek just like a boat. Hebert took Martha Mae Bear's paw and away they went to see where the stick would go. They ran and ran on their little fat legs down the creek. Soon they were nowhere to be seen. Oscar Bear was sound asleep. He was supposed to watch the bear babies, but he just kept right on sleeping.

Oscar Bear: "Snore, snore, snore."

Storyteller: Geraldene Bear was busy washing the dirty clothes and she didn't notice the bear babies were gone

Oscar Bear: "Oh, oh, oh! Something's got me."

Storyteller: Poor old Oscar Bear didn't know what had him. He just kep on yelling as loud as he could!

Oscar Bear: "Help! Help! Help! Help me, Geraldene."

Storyteller: Geraldene Bear heard Oscar and she came running. She saw right away that it was just a fish that had Oscar.

Geraldene Bear: "Now, Oscar, you just quit that hollering and I'll help you catch that fish."

Storyteller: So Geraldene Bear and Oscar Bear pulled as hard as they could.

Oscar Bear & Geraldene Bear: "Uh, uh, uh, uh, uh, uh, uh."

Storyteller: They caught that big fish. Oscar Bear rubbed his tummy and said:

Oscar Bear: "My, my, what a good lunch we'll have."

Storyteller: Just then, Geraldene Bear missed the little bear babies. She said:

Geraldene Bear: "Oh, where are my babies? Where are Little Hebert and Martha Mae Bear?"

Storyteller: Poor Geraldene was really upset! The bear babies were nowhere to be seen. Oscar Bear and Geraldene Bear ran up the creek but the babies weren't there. They ran down the creek. They ran and ran until they were huffing and puffing.

Oscar Bear & Geraldene Bear: "Huff, huff, huff."

Storyteller: Finally, there they were! There were Little Hebert and Martha Mae Bear! They were sitting on the bank of the creek making mud pies. Oh, those little bears! They were so muddy. They had mud pies all over them!

Geraldene Bear and Oscar Bear were so glad to see the bear babies that they picked them up and gave them great big bear hugs. Well then, you know what happened? Geraldene Bear and Oscar Bear got mud pies all over them just like the bear babies. What muddy bears! They didn't care because they had found Little Hebert and Martha Mae Bear.

The bears went back up the creek where Geraldene Bear had been washing the dirty clothes. They jumped in the nice clean water. "Kersplash!" Geraldene Bear sprinkled Bubble-O all over them. Pretty soon the creek was full of bubbles and clean bears.

The bear babies were tired by then. They yawned big yawns and rubbed their sleepy eyes.

Bear Babies: (Yawn and rub eyes.)

Storyteller: Geraldene Bear carried Martha Mae Bear and the clean clothes and Oscar Bear carried Little Hebert and the big fish and they all went home for lunch.

Oscar Bear cooked the big fish while Geraldene Bear put the bear babies' nice clean nighties on them. (Put nighties on bear babies.) Then they all ate the fish for lunch and licked their bowls clean.

Bear: "Slurp, slurp, slurp."

Storyteller: There were now four sleepy bears. Oscar Bear and Geraldene Bear yawned and yawned and rubbed their sleepy eyes.

Bears: "Yawn, yawn." (Rub eyes.)

Storyteller: They took the bear babies in their room and put them in their little beds. (Put bear babies in bed.) They covered them up and kissed them "nightie night" like this:

Bear: "Smack, smack."

Storyteller: Then Oscar Bear and Geraldene Bear climbed into their own bed and went to sleep.

Bears: "Snore, snore."

Storyteller: (in a whisper) All the bears were sound asleep.

Bears: (softly) "Snore, snore, snore."

Storyteller: (in a whisper) "Shhh! Don't wake them up.

THE WRECK

Storyteller: One day at the bears' pretty little house in the woods the sun was shining brightly. It was very, very hot. Little Hebert said:

Little Hebert: "I am hot. I am as hot as a firecracker."

Storyteller: Martha Mae Bear said:

Martha Mae Bear: "I'm hot too. I am about to burn up."

Storyteller: Geraldene Bear said:

Geraldene Bear: "Oh my poor little baby bears are SO hot. Oscar Bear, why don't we take these baby bears to the creek to cool off?"

Storyteller: Oscar Bear said:

Oscar Bear: ""Oh, yes, let's all go to the creek. We can swim in the nice cool water. The babies can take their little buckets and shovels and play in the sand, too."

Storyteller: So the bears all put on their bathing suits. Since it was so hot, the bears decided to ride in their van to the creek. Martha Mae Bear climbed into her car seat. Oscar Bear buckled her in. Little Hebert said:

Little Hebert: "I don't want to fasten my seat belt today, but I will sit very still."

Storyteller: Little Hebert sat very still in the back seat. Geraldene Bear got in the driver's seat and buckled her seat belt. Oscar Bear sat by Geraldene in the front seat. He buckled his seat belt and away the bears went in their van to the creek. "Chug, chug, chug" went their van. Well, they were almost there when a terrible thing happened! A bee flew into the van. It buzzed 'round and 'round Geraldene's head! "Buzz, buzz!" Poor Geraldene got so excited about the bee that she forgot to drive the van.

Geraldene Bear: "Oh, oh! Get that bee out of here"

Storyteller: The van ran off the road and crashed into a tree. BANG!! Well, poor Little Hebert was thrown out of the van because he wasn't buckled in his car seat. He cried and cried.

Little Hebert: "Oh, my arm hurts. My poor little arm is broken."

Storyteller: Geraldene and Oscar quickly unbuckled their seat belts and jumped out of the van. They ran over to Little Hebert. They looked at his arm. Geraldene said:

Geraldene Bear: "Now , now, Little Hebert, your arm is not broken. It is just scratched."

Storyteller: Geraldene wrapped his arm up in bandages and gave him a kiss. "Smack." Oscar gave him a kiss, too. "Smack."

Little Hebert stopped crying. The bears got back into their van and buckled their seatbelts. This time Little Hebert got in his car seat and Oscar buckled him in. Away they went again in their van. "Chug, chug, chug." When they came to the creek, Geraldene, Oscar, and Martha Mae Bear jumped into the creek. "Kersplash!" Geraldene Bear said:

Geraldene Bear: "Little Hebert, I am sorry you cannot get in the creek. You might get your bandage wet."

Storyteller: So Little Hebert played in the sand with his bucket and shovel. Geraldene, Oscar, and Martha Mae Bear splashed in the water and had lots of fun. Finally the bears got tired. They got back into their van and they all buckled up so they would be safe. Even Little Hebert. The tired bears chugged away home in their van to their pretty little house in the woods.

GOLDILOCKS AND THE THREE BEARS

Storyteller: Once upon a time there were three bears. There was a great big bear who was named Oscar Bear. There was a middle-sized bear who was named Geraldene Bear. And there was a little tiny bear who was named Hebert. One morning, Geraldene Bear made porridge for breakfast. She called Oscar Bear and Little Hebert.

Geraldene Bear: "Breakfast is ready."

Storyteller: The bears sat down to eat their porridge. Oscar Bear tasted his porridge and said:

Oscar Bear: "Oh, this porridge is too hot."

Storyteller: Geraldene Bear tasted her porridge and said:

Geraldene Bear: "Oh, this porridge is too hot."

Storyteller: Little Hebert tasted his porridge and said:

Little Hebert: "Ooooh, ooooh, this porridge is too hot! It burned my little mouth."

Storyteller: Geraldene Bear said:

Geraldene Bear: "Now, now, Little Hebert. Don't cry. We'll go for a walk in the woods and when we come back the porridge will be just right."

Storyteller: So the bears left their porridge on the table to cool and went for a walk in the woods. Just after the bears had left, a little girl named Goldilocks came along. She saw the bears' pretty little house and she tip-toed right up to the door. She didn't hear anyone inside so she opened the door and went in. Goldilocks saw the bears' porridge on the table and she was hungry, so she sat right down and tasted Oscar Bear's big bowl of porridge.

Goldilocks: "Ooooh this porridge is too salty."

Storyteller: Then she tasted Geraldene Bear's middle-sized bowl of porridge and she said:

Goldilocks: "Ooooh, this porridge is too sweet."

Storyteller: Then she tasted Little Hebert's tiny bowl of porridge and she said:

Goldilocks: "Yummy, yummy! This porridge is just right."

Storyteller: And Goldilocks ate up all of Little Hebert's porridge. Then Goldilocks went into the living room where she saw three chairs, a great big chair, a middle-sized chair and a little tiny chair. She sat down in Oscar Bear's great big chair and said,

Goldilocks: "Oooh, this chair is too hard."

Storyteller: Then Goldilocks sat down in Geraldene Bear's middle-sized chair and said:

Goldilocks: "Ooooh, this chair is too soft."

Storyteller: Then Goldilocks sat down in Little Hebert's tiny chair and said:

Goldilocks: "This little chair is just right."

Storyteller: And Goldilocks rocked and rocked in the little chair. Then she rocked too hard and the little chair broke all to pieces and Goldilocks fell on the floor.

Goldilocks: "Bad chair. That hurt."

Storyteller: Then Goldilocks went upstairs where she saw three beds, a great big bed, a middle-sized bed and a little tiny bed. She laid down on Oscar Bear's great big bed and said:

Goldilocks: "Oooh, this bed is too hard."

Storyteller: Then Goldilocks laid down on Geraldene Bear's middle-sized bed and said:

Goldilocks: Oooh, this bed is too soft."

Storyteller: Then Goldilocks laid down on Little Hebert's little tiny bed and said:

Goldilocks: "This little bed is just right."

Storyteller: And Goldilocks went fast asleep. Pretty soon the bears came back from their walk in the woods. They went into the kitchen to eat their porridge. Oscar Bear said:

Oscar Bear: "Somebody's been eating my porridge!"

Storyteller: Geraldene Bear said:

Geraldene Bear: "Somebody's been eating my porridge."

Storyteller: And Little Hebert said:

Little Hebert: "Somebody's been eating my porridge and they ate it all up! Wah, Wah, Wah."

Storyteller: Little Hebert cried and cried. Geraldene Bear said:

Geraldene Bear: "Now, now, Little Hebert. Don't cry. Let's go in the living room and see if we can find who ate up your porridge."

Storyteller: And so the bears went into the living room. Oscar Bear said:

Oscar Bear: "Somebody's been sitting in my chair."

Storyteller: Geraldene Bear said:

Geraldene Bear: Somebody's been sitting in my chair!"

Storyteller: And Little Hebert said:

Little Hebert: "Somebody's been sitting in my chair and they broke it all to pieces. Wah, Wah, Wah."

Storyteller: Little Hebert sat down on the floor and kicked his heels and cried. Geraldene Bear said:

Geraldene Bear: "Now, now, Little Hebert, don't cry. We'll go upstairs and see if we can catch that person who ate your porridge and broke your little chair."

Storyteller: And so the bears all went upstairs. Oscar Bear said:

Oscar Bear: "Somebody's been sleeping in my bed."

Storyteller: And Geraldene Bear said:

Geraldene Bear: "Somebody's been sleeping in my bed."

Storyteller: And Little Hebert said:

Little Hebert: "Somebody's been sleeping in my bed and there she is!"

Storyteller: Little Hebert yelled so loud that he woke up Goldilocks. She was scared to death and she jumped out of the window and ran all the way home. Goldilocks never did come back to the bears' house.

HEBERT VISITS GOLDILOCKS

Storyteller: One day Goldilocks' mama baked goodies for Grandma, who was sick. She put all the goodies, except a big chocolate cake, in a basket to take to Grandma. She left the cake on the table so they could eat it for supper. Then away went Goldilocks and her mama to visit Grandma.

Well, along came Little Hebert, who was out picking flowers. He saw some pretty purple thistles in Goldilocks' yard and he went right in the yard and picked them all. Then he tip-toed up to the door to peek inside. The door came open and he went into the house.

There, on the kitchen table, was the biggest chocolate cake Little Hebert had ever seen. He was very hungry, so he sat down and ate the cake all up, every last crumb of it. Well, bears have terrible table manners and they don't ever use napkins, so Little Hebert got chocolate cake all over his face and his paws and even on his fat little belly.

Then he went into the living room and saw three chairs. He sat down on Goldilocks' Papa's big chair and got chocolate cake all over it. He said:

Little Hebert: "Oooooh, this chair is too big for me."

Storyteller: Then Little Hebert sat down in Goldilocks' Mama's middle-sized chair and got chocolate cake all over it. He said:

Little Hebert: "Ooooooh, this chair is too soft for me."

Storyteller: Then Little Hebert sat down in Goldilocks' little chair. He said:

Little Hebert: "This little chair is just my size."

Storyteller: Little Hebert began to rock in Goldilocks' little chair. He rocked faster and faster and all at once the little chair broke all to pieces and Little Hebert fell on the floor.

Little Hebert decided to go upstairs and he saw three beds. He tried Goldilocks' Papa's big bed and got chocolate cake all over it. He said:

Little Hebert: "Ooooooh, this bed is too big."

Storyteller: Then Little Hebert tried Goldilocks' Mama's middle-sized bed and got chocolate cake all over it. He said:

Little Hebert: "Ooooh, this bed is too soft."

Storyteller: Then Little Hebert tried Goldilocks' little bed and got chocolate cake all over it. Soon he was fast asleep.

Pretty soon Goldilocks and her Mama came home. Goldilocks' Mama took one look at where her beautiful chocolate cake had been and said:

Goldilocks' Mama: "Somebody ate our chocolate cake and it's all gone."

Storyteller: They went into the livingroom. Goldilocks' Mama said:

Goldilocks' Mama: "Somebody sat in Papa's big chair and got chocolate cake all over it, and somebody sat in my middle-sized chair and got chocolate cake all over it."

Storyteller: Goldilocks said:

Goldilocks: "Somebody sat in my little chair and got chocolate cake all over it and broke it all to pieces."

Storyteller: Goldilocks began to cry.

Goldilocks: "Boo, hoo! My little chair is broken all to pieces."

Storyteller: She cried so loud that she woke Little Hebert up. He had never heard such carrying on and he was scared to death. He jumped out of the window and ran all the way home. Goldilocks and her Mama went upstairs.

Goldilocks' Mama: Somebody laid down on Papa's big bed and got chocolate cake all over it. Somebody laid down on my middle-sized bed and got chocolate cake all over it, too.

Storyteller: And Goldilocks said:

Goldilocks: "Somebody laid down on my little bed and got chocolate cake all over it."

Storyteller: Goldilocks' Mama said:

Goldilocks' Mama: "I declare! Who could have made all this mess?"

Goldilocks: "Maybe it was a bear."

Storyteller: Goldilocks' Mama said:

Goldilocks' Mama: "Why, Goldilocks, what does a little girl like you know about bears?"

Goldilocks: "Well, one time I went to visit the bears."

Storyteller: Goldilocks' Mama said:

Goldilocks' Mama: "Now Goldilocks! Little girls mustn't tell stories."

But we know Goldilocks wasn't telling a story. She really did go to visit the bears one time, didn't she?

GERALDENE AND OSCAR'S HOUSE

MATERIALS:
—One 9 X 12 inch piece bright yellow felt
—Scraps of bright pink, rust, white, green, blue, and black felt
—Fourteen inches of medium white rick-rack
—One 4-inch square of plastic wrap
—Thin line permanent black marking pen

DIRECTIONS:
Using house pattern, cut one house from gold felt. Cut out window. Cut door on three sides so that it opens. Cut shutters from pink felt and glue at sides of windows. Cut window box from white felt and glue at bottom of window. Cut small flower shapes from felt and place in window box.

Cut small heart shape from pink felt and glue on door. Cut doorknob from black felt and glue on door.

Using chimney pattern, cut one chimney from rust felt and glue behind house on roof. Cut two strips of rick-rack the length of the roof pieces. Cut two roof pieces from pink scraps. Glue rick-rack on top of roof pieces on lower edge of roof. Glue roof in place.

Put window in the house using the instructions given for window in the "Three Little Pigs."

GRANNIE BEAR'S HOUSE

MATERIALS:
—One 9 X 12 inch piece of bright pink felt
—Scraps of blue, red, brown, white felt
—Fourteen inches of 1-inch gathered white eyelet trim

DIRECTIONS:
Using pattern, cut one house shape from the bright pink felt.

Cut along dotted lines of window and fold shutters back. Glue open. Cut two small blue hearts and glue to shutters. Cut one white window box and several flowers. Glue to the bottom of the window. Cut one red heart to glue on window box. Cut doorknob from brown felt and glue to door.

Cut two roof shapes from blue felt. Glue eyelet so that it shows under the edge of the roof.

Cut one chimney shape and glue to the back edge of roof so that it shows above the roof.

Put window in house using the instructions given in "Three Little Pigs."

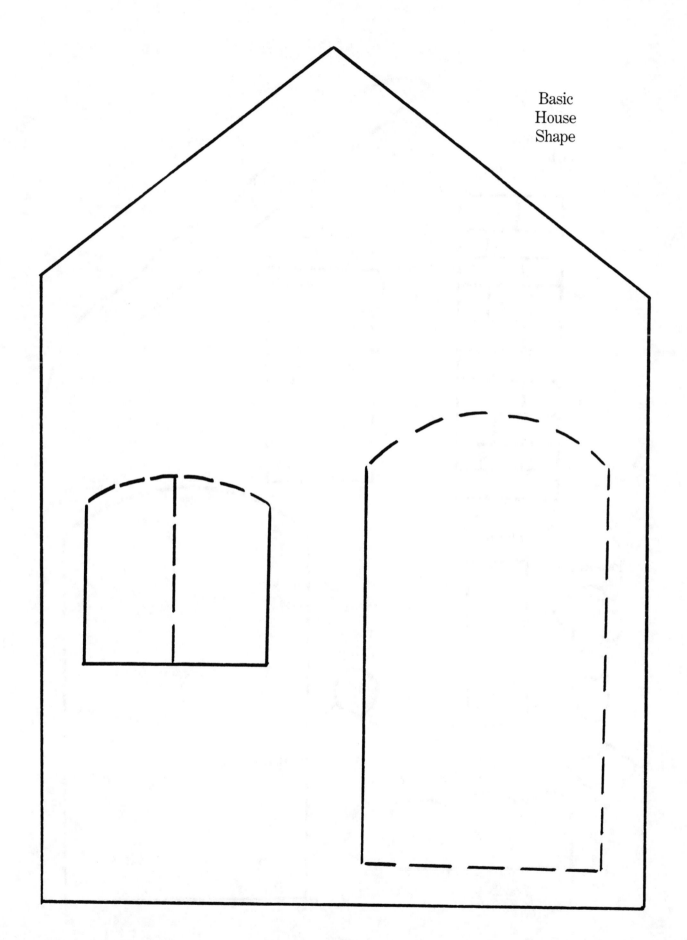

Basic
House
Shape

37

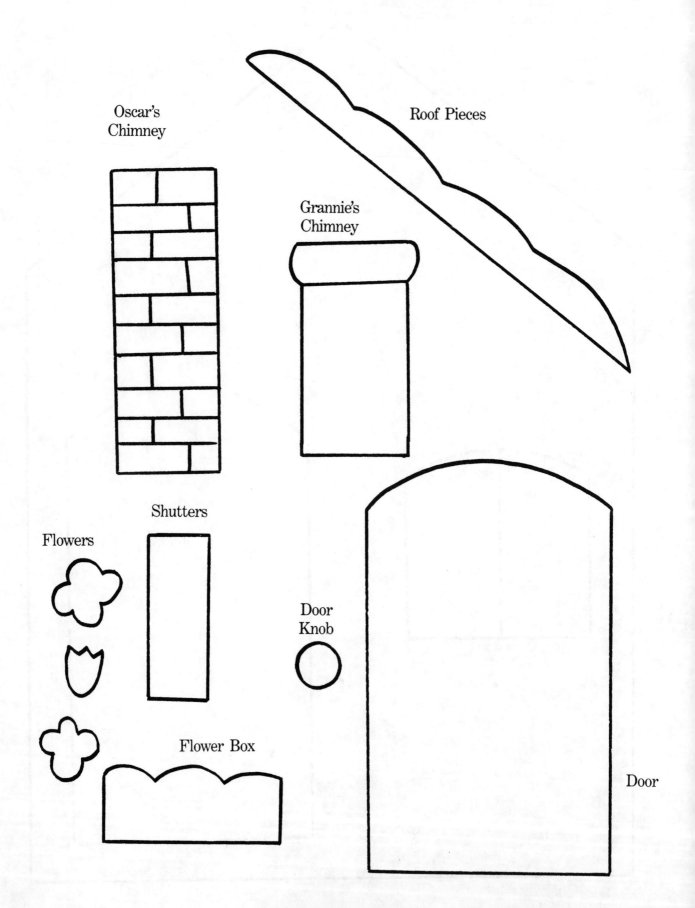

Oscar's
Chimney

Roof Pieces

Grannie's
Chimney

Shutters

Flowers

Door
Knob

Flower Box

Door

38

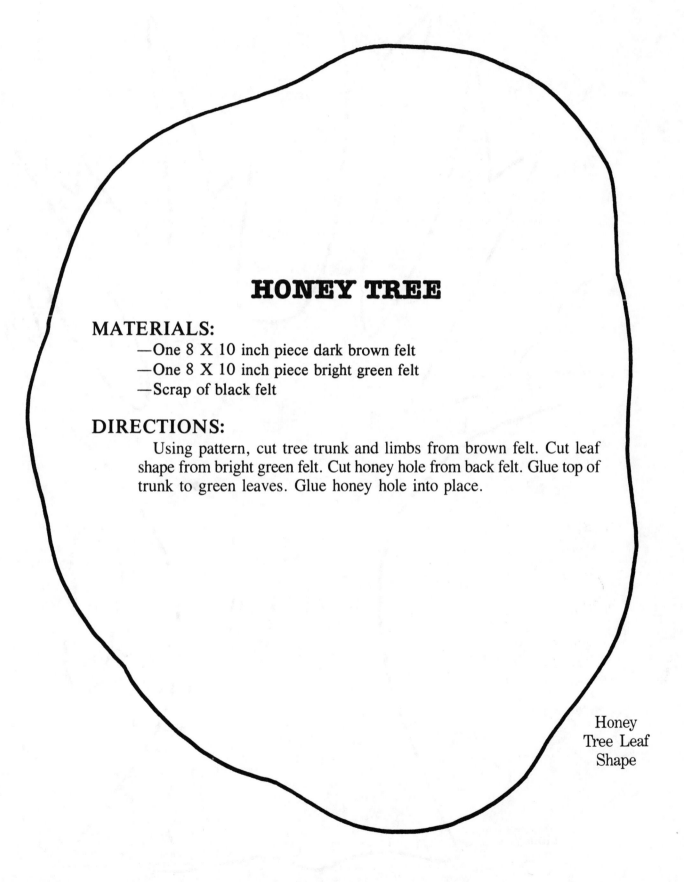

HONEY TREE

MATERIALS:
—One 8 X 10 inch piece dark brown felt
—One 8 X 10 inch piece bright green felt
—Scrap of black felt

DIRECTIONS:
Using pattern, cut tree trunk and limbs from brown felt. Cut leaf shape from bright green felt. Cut honey hole from back felt. Glue top of trunk to green leaves. Glue honey hole into place.

Honey
Tree Leaf
Shape

Honey
Tree

40

CREEK

MATERIALS:
- One 8" X 4" piece of blue felt
- Scraps of tan and green felt
- Blue glitter

DIRECTIONS:
Using the creek pattern, cut creek from blue felt. Cut 3½" slit in the creek so that fish can be pulled from, and Geraldene can get into, creek. Draw waves with glue and sprinkle with blue glitter. Let dry, then shake off excess glitter. Using the grass pattern, cut sprigs of grass from green felt and glue around the outer edge of the creek. Cut rock shapes from the tan felt and glue on the outer edge of the creek.

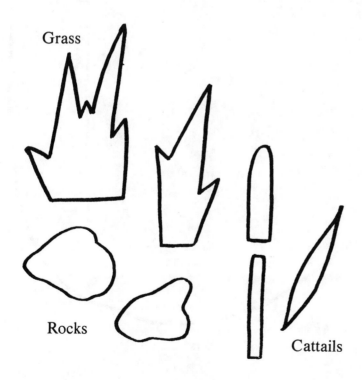

Grass

Rocks

Cattails

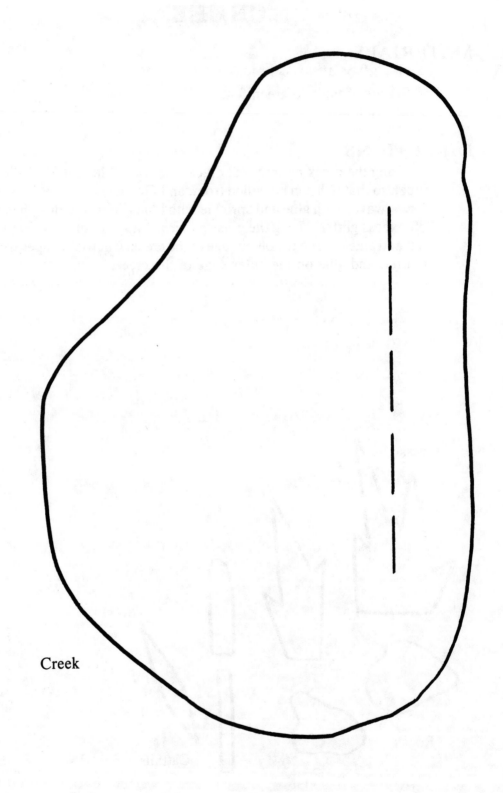

Creek

MUDHOLE

Mudhole

MATERIALS:
—One 8" X 6" piece of brown felt
—Scraps of tan and green felt

DIRECTIONS:
Using mudhole pattern, cut mudhole from brown felt. Cut a slit 5½" as shown by dotted line. Using grass clump pattern, cut grass and glue clumps around the mudhole. Cut rock shapes from tan felt and glue around edge of mudhole.

Cattails   Rocks   Grass

CLOUDS

MATERIALS:
—One 9 X 12 inch piece white felt

DIRECTIONS:
Cut cloud shapes from white felt. Place as directed on the flannel-board.

Cloud

GERALDENE BEAR

MATERIALS:
—One 4 X 8 inch piece tan felt
—One 4 X 4 inch piece pink felt
—Scraps of red, white, yellow, brown, and green felt
—T̶o 10mm wiggle eyes
   ̶o small snaps
   ̶ 5mm black pom-pom
   ̶ ½-inch red pom-pom
   ̶dle and tan thread
   ̶nanent fine line black marker

̶ONS:
 ̶sing pattern for large bear, cut body and two arms from tan felt. Cut
 ̶raldene's overalls from pink felt, two heart pockets from red felt, and
 ̶zzle from dark brown felt.

 ̶Glue pockets to overalls. Glue muzzle onto bear's face, then glue
 ̶ck pom-pom nose to muzzle. Glue eyes in place. Glue overalls to
 ̶.

 ̶ snaps to bear's shoulder and top of arm. The arms should be on
 ̶nt of the bear, and will move over the overalls.

 ̶wo flowers from scraps of felt and glue on top of Geraldene's
 ̶ark ears, stitching, and toes with black marking pen.

 ̶: The red pom-pom is used with a doubled piece of masking
tape to ̶̶̶ck to Geraldene's nose when she is stung by the bees.)

OSCAR BEAR

MATERIALS:
—One 4 X 8 inch piece tan felt
—Two 10mm wiggle eyes
—Two small snaps
—One 5mm black pom-pom
—Needle and tan thread
—Permanent fine line black marker

DIRECTIONS:
Using bear pattern, cut one large body and two arms from tan felt. Cut overalls from blue felt. Glue a scrap of red felt behind neck of overalls so that it looks like a shirt.

Cut muzzle from brown felt and glue in place. Glue black pom-pom nose on muzzle. Glue overalls to bear body.

Fasten arms to body with snaps in the same manner that Geraldene's are put on.

Make details of ears, stitching, and toes with black marking pen.

Oscar

Geraldene

46

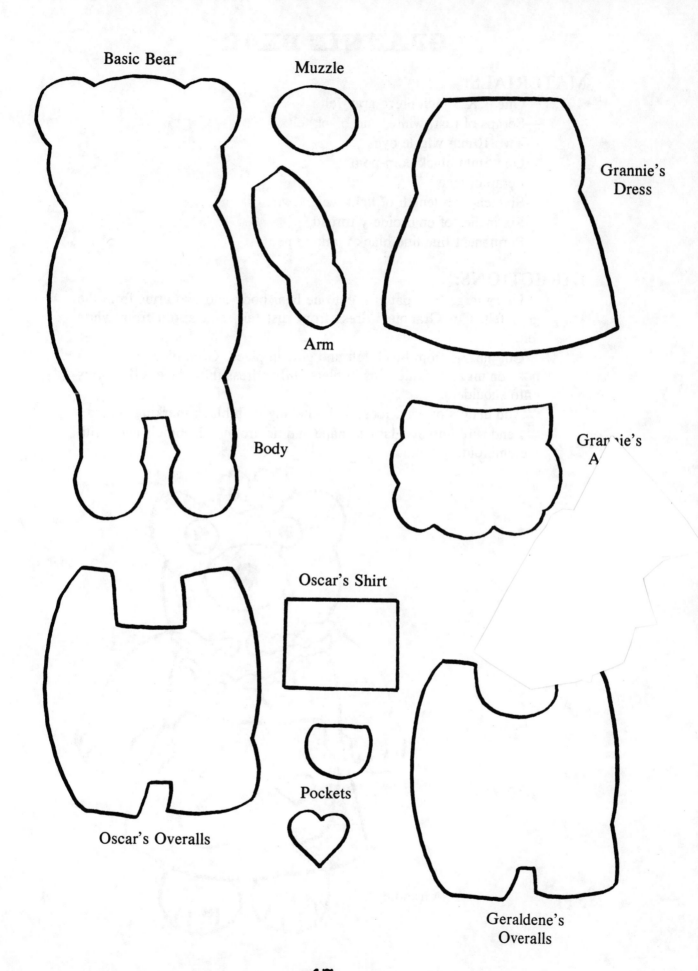

Basic Bear

Muzzle

Grannie's
Dress

Arm

Body

Grannie's
A

Oscar's Shirt

Pockets

Oscar's Overalls

Geraldene's
Overalls

GRANNIE BEAR

MATERIALS:

— One 4 X 8 inch piece gray felt
— Scraps of rust, white, and black felt
— Two 10mm wiggle eyes
— One 5mm black pom-pom
— Scrap of lace
— Sixteen-inch length of light-weight wire
— Six inches of embroidery thread
— Permanent fine line black marking pen

DIRECTIONS:

Using large bear pattern, cut one bear body and two arms from the gray felt. Cut Grannie's dress from rust felt, and apron from white felt.

Cut muzzle from black felt and glue in place. Glue black pom-pom nose on muzzle. Glue eyes in place. Glue dress into place. Glue arms onto shoulders.

Add details of ears, toes, and stitching with black marking pen.

Bend wire into eyeglasses shape and tie around Grannie's neck with the embroidery thread.

Grannie

LITTLE HEBERT

MATERIALS:
- —4 X 5 inch piece of tan felt
- —Scraps of brown, light blue, yellow felt
- —Two 10 mm wiggle eyes
- —One 5 mm black pom-pom
- —Permanent fine line black marker

DIRECTIONS:
Using pattern, cut Little Hebert and his arms from tan felt. Cut muzzle from black felt. Cut overalls from blue felt, and pockets and hat from yellow felt. Glue pockets to overalls, then glue overalls to body. Glue arms over overalls at shoulders.

Glue muzzle and black pom-pom nose to bear's face. Glue eyes in place.

Add ear, toe, and stitching details with black marking pen. Glue hat on head after drawing features.

MARTHA MAE BEAR

MATERIALS:
- —One 3 X 4 inch piece tan felt
- —Scraps of white and brown felt
- —Two 6 mm wiggle eyes
- —Six inches ⅛-inch pink ribbon
- —Tiny gold safety pin

DIRECTIONS:
Using pattern, cut one body and two arms from tan felt. Cut muzzle from brown felt and diaper from white felt. Glue diaper and arms into place (be sure to glue arms on front of bear). Glue muzzle and pom-pom nose into place. Glue eyes into place.

Add ear detail, toes, and stitching marks with black marking pen.

Glue bow made from the ribbon on top of head. Fasten safety pin on the diaper.

Martha
Mae

Hebert

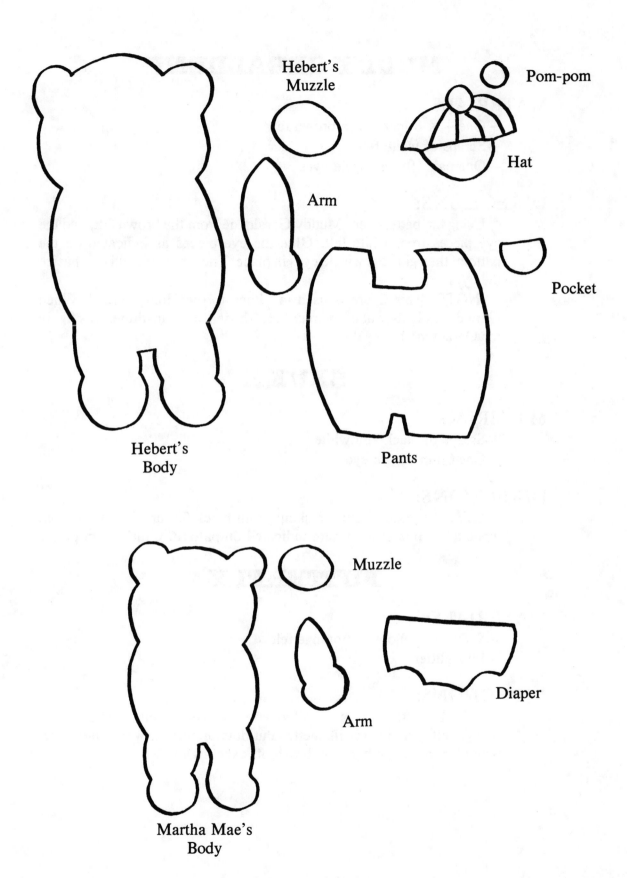

Hebert's
Muzzle

Pom-pom

Arm

Hat

Pocket

Hebert's
Body

Pants

Muzzle

Arm

Diaper

Martha Mae's
Body

MUDDY GERALDENE

MATERIALS:
—One 4 X 8 inch piece brown felt
—Scraps of white felt
—One pair 10mm wiggle eyes

DIRECTIONS:
Using the pattern, cut Muddy Geraldene from the brown felt, and the eye pieces from white felt. Glue the eye pieces as indicated on the pattern, then glue the wiggle eyes in place. The white felt will emphasize the eyes.

(NOTE: This figure is used in "Back to the Honey Tree." When Geraldene climbs out of the mudhole, the teacher substitutes this figure for Geraldene.)

SKUNK

MATERIALS:
—Scraps of black and white felt
—One 6mm wiggle eye

DIRECTIONS:
Using the pattern, cut the skunk from black felt and his stripe from white felt. Glue stripe where indicated on pattern. Glue eye in place.

BUTTERFLY

MATERIALS:
—Scraps of yellow and orange felt
—Blue glitter

DIRECTIONS:
Using butterfly pattern, cut silhouette from yellow felt. Cut body from orange felt and glue to silhouette. Put dots of glue on wings and cover with blue glitter. When dry, brush off excess glitter.

Muddy Geraldene

Butterfly

Eyes

Skunk

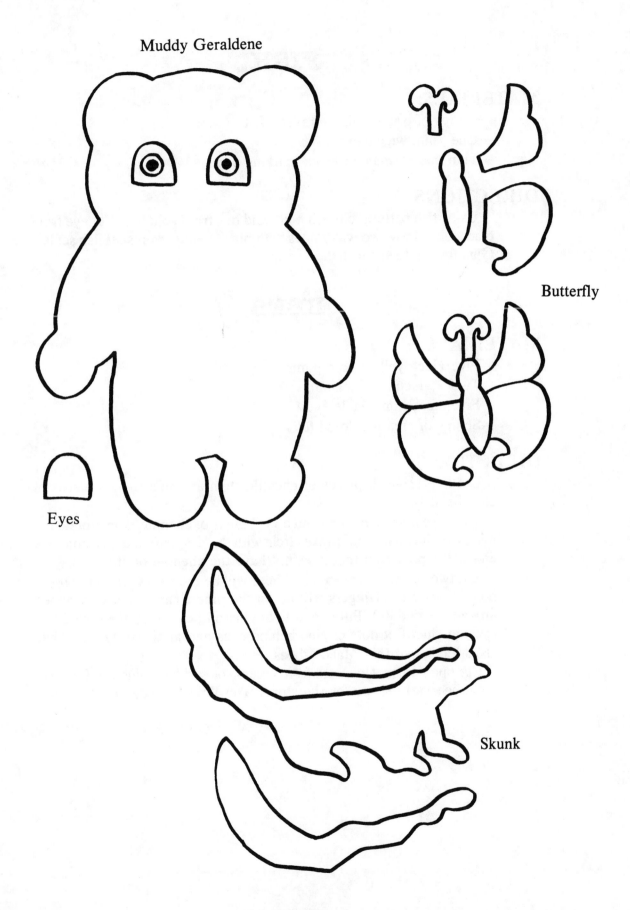

FISH

MATERIALS:

—Scraps of bright gold and black felt
—One 5 mm wiggle eye
—Thin line permanent black marking pen

DIRECTIONS:

Using fish pattern, cut fish body and fins from gold felt. Cut eye from black felt. Draw two wavy lines with black pen to represent fish scales. Glue fins and eyes to fish.

BEES

MATERIALS:

—Five 1 inch yellow pom-poms
—Two 12-inch black chenille stems
—Five pair 3 mm wiggle eyes
—Scraps of cream-colored felt

DIRECTIONS:

Cut five 1¼-inch pieces of chenille stem and five ½-inch pieces of chenille stem.

Take one pom-pom and bend a 1¼" piece of chenille stem around the middle of the pom-pom. Make circle with the ½" piece and glue onto one end of the pom-pom that does not have the chenille on it.

Cut two ¼" circles from felt. These will be the wings. Hold the pom-pom by the sides (fingers will be on the pipe cleaner that is wrapped around the middle). Put two dots of glue on pom-pom, then put 3 mm eyes on glue. Put dots of glue behind eyes and attach wings. The bee should look like this. Make 5 bees.

Cut one swarm silhouette from cream colored felt. Glue the five bees onto the swarm shape for the story "The Wreck," make one bee as directed.

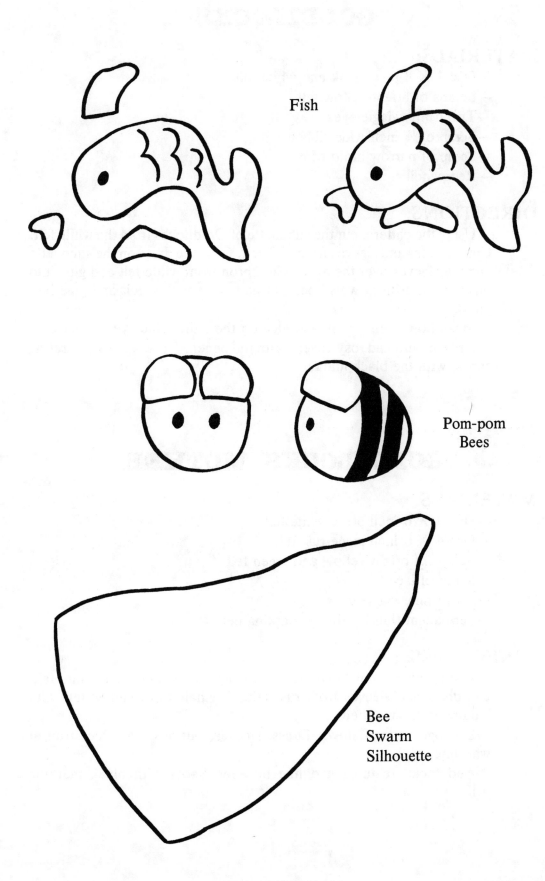

Fish

Pom-pom
Bees

Bee
Swarm
Silhouette

55

GOLDILOCKS

MATERIALS:
- —One 4 X 8 piece pink and white felt
- —Scraps of bright yellow felt
- —Two 6 mm wiggle eyes
- —Scrap of ⅛-inch-wide ribbon
- —Scrap of narrow braid trim
- —Red pencil

DIRECTIONS:
Using the pattern, cut the silhouette of Goldilocks from the white felt. Cut the dress and sleeves from pink felt. Glue the dress on the silhouette and the sleeves over the arms. Cut apron from white felt and glue into place. Glue trim at waistline. Cut hair from yellow felt and glue into place.

Make bow from ribbon and glue on the hair. Glue eyes in place.

Draw mouth and rosy cheeks with red pencil. Draw a line, separating shoes, with the black marker.

GOLDILOCKS' MOTHER

MATERIALS:
- —One 4 X 6 inch piece white felt
- —One 4 X 6 inch piece rust felt
- —Scraps of bright yellow and green felt
- —Scrap of lace trim
- —Two 6 mm wiggle eyes
- —Permanent thin line black marking pen

DIRECTIONS:
Using pattern, cut Goldilocks' Mother's silhouette from white felt. Cut dress and sleeves from rust felt. Cut hair from yellow felt. Cut buttons from green felt.

Put together as follows: Dress, sleeves, buttons, hair, lace trim at waistline, eyes.

Add facial features and line between boots with black marking pen.

Shoes

Hair

Goldilocks

Arms
(Cut 2)

Apron

Dress

57

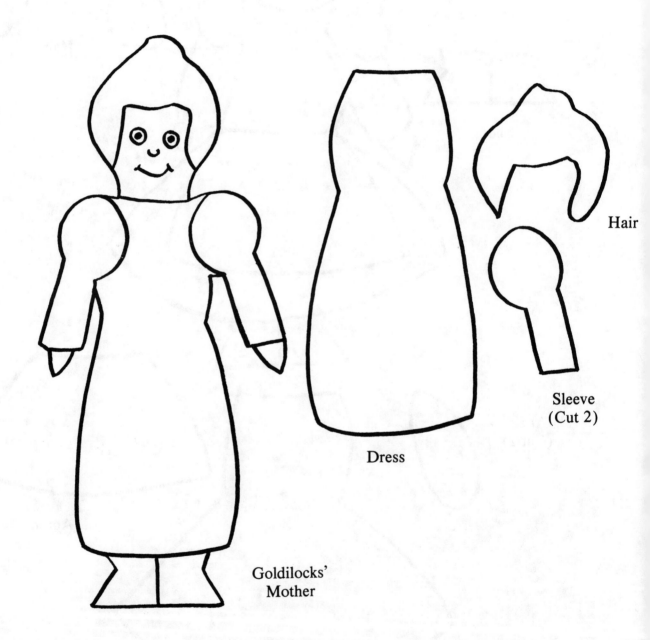

Hair

Sleeve
(Cut 2)

Dress

Goldilocks'
Mother

CHAIRS

MATERIALS:
—One 9 X 12 inch piece of tan felt
—Scrap of red felt

DIRECTIONS:
Using patterns, cut the three chairs from tan felt and the chair cushion for Mama's chair from red felt. Glue cushion to middle-sized chair.

(NOTE: The chairs are used in the "Three Bears" and "Goldilocks Visits Hebert.")

TABLE

MATERIALS:
—One 4 X 8 inch piece tan felt
—Thin line permanent black marking pen

DIRECTIONS:
Cut the table from tan felt, using the table pattern.

The table is used in "The Three Bears" and "Hebert Visits Goldilocks."

BOWLS

MATERIALS:
—Scraps of white, orange, green, and red felt

DIRECTIONS:
Cut porridge from white felt, and three bowls from the other scraps. Glue porridge to bowls.

CAKE

MATERIALS:
—Scraps of yellow and pink felt
—Permanent black marking pen

DIRECTIONS:
Cut the cake from pink felt and the plate from yellow felt. Glue cake to plate. Add details with black marking pen.

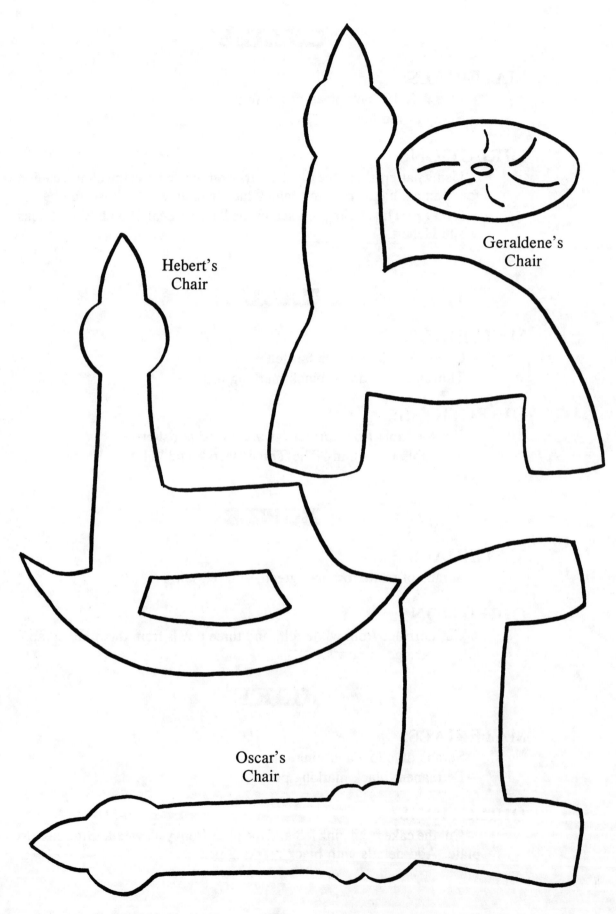

Hebert's
Chair

Geraldene's
Chair

Oscar's
Chair

60

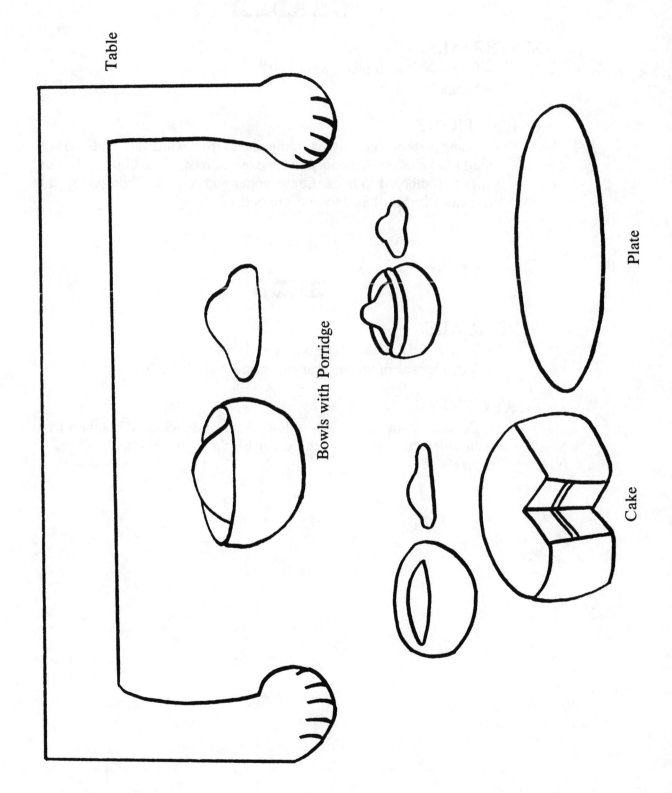

Table

Plate

Bowls with Porridge

Cake

61

CRADLE

MATERIALS:
—One 4 X 8 inch piece white felt
—Scraps pink felt

DIRECTIONS:
Using pattern, cut the two cradle pieces from white felt. Cut two pink hearts and glue one to headboard and one to footboard. Glue rocker and sides of footboard to back. Leave upper end of footboard open so that you can slip Martha Mae into the bed.

BEDS

MATERIALS:
—Two 9 X 12 inch pieces bright yellow felt
—Large scraps of white, orange, green, and blue felt

DIRECTIONS:
Cut beds from yellow felt, pillows from white felt, and blankets from orange, green, and blue felt. Glue blankets to beds and pillows to blankets.

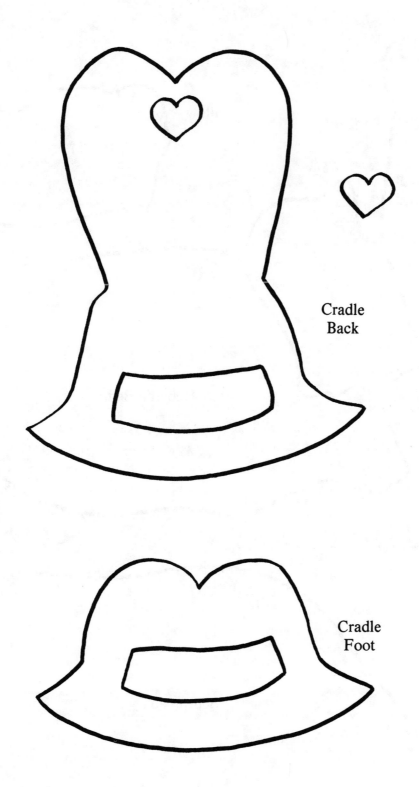

Cradle
Back

Cradle
Foot

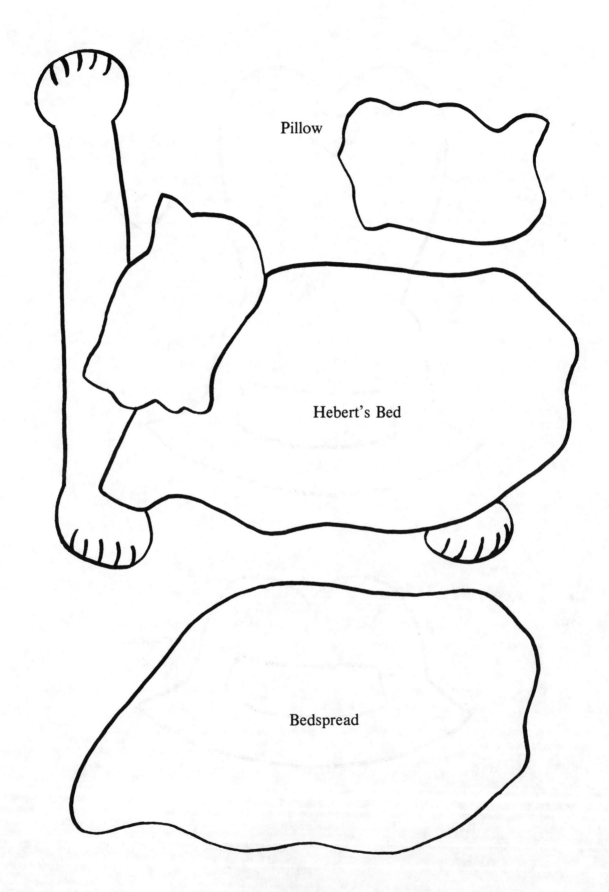

Pillow

Hebert's Bed

Bedspread

64

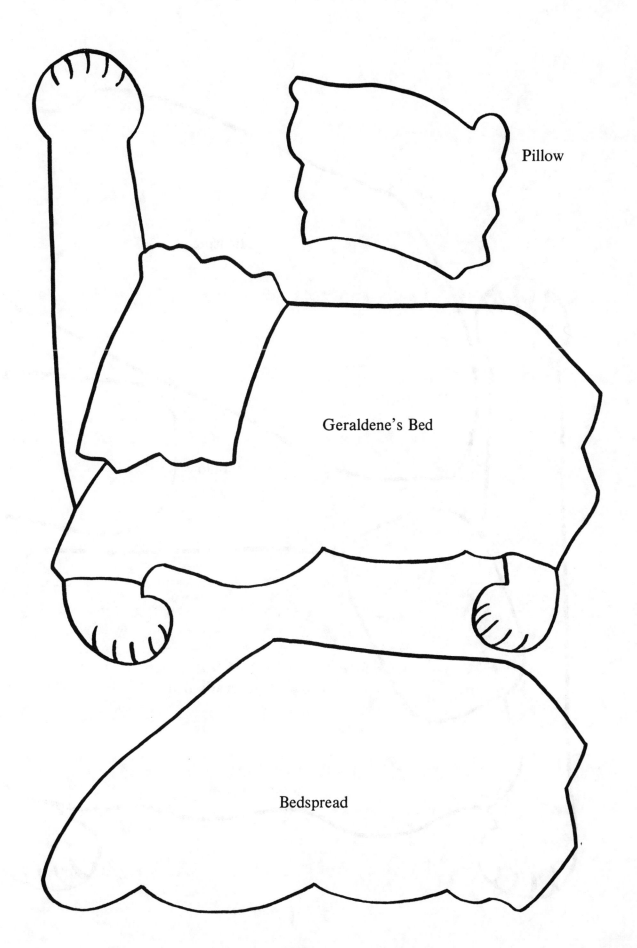

Pillow

Geraldene's Bed

Bedspread

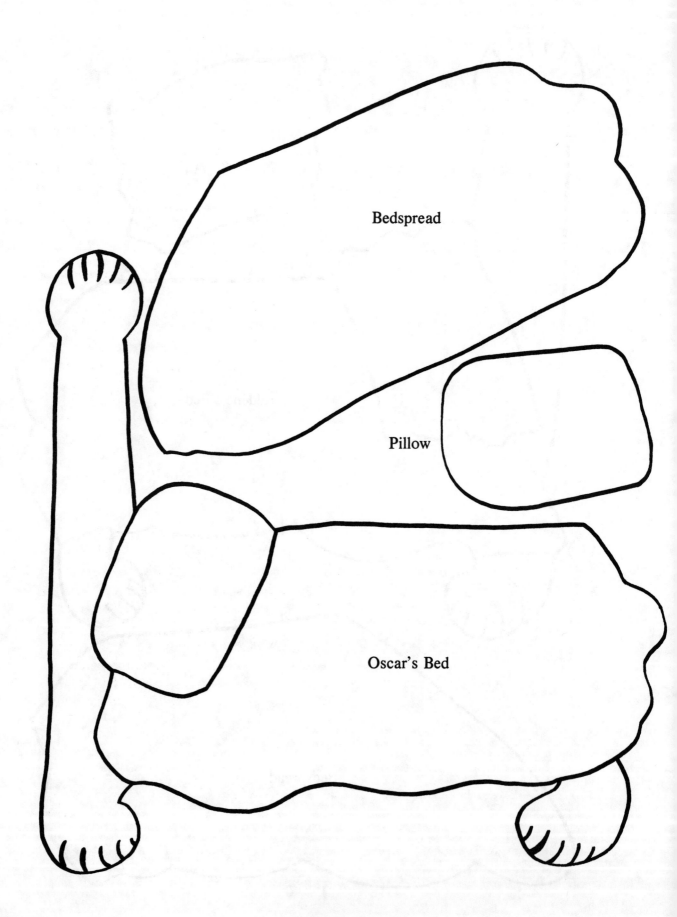

Bedspread

Pillow

Oscar's Bed

GERALDENE AND OSCAR'S VAN

MATERIALS:
—Two 9 X 12 inch pieces gray felt
—One 9 X 12 inch piece turquoise felt
—One 4 X 6 inch piece black felt
—One 4 X 6 inch piece light blue felt
—Scraps of gold felt
—One 4 X 8 inch piece plastic wrap

DIRECTIONS:

Using patterns, cut one gray silhouette of back of van which will serve as a base for attaching all other parts. Cut Geraldene's, Oscar's, Hebert's, and Martha Mae's seats from blue felt. Cut seat belts from black felt. Cut slits on silhouette as indicated on the pattern. Glue the four seats and seat belts above the appropriate slits. (Oscar and Geraldene's seats are glued above the two lower slits. Hebert's seat is glued above the upper right slit and Martha Mae's above the upper left slit.) Put a drop of glue on the seats as indicated on the pattern and place one end of seatbelt in glue and press.

Cut one silhouette for front of van from turquoise felt. Cut windshield, hood, and fenders from turquoise felt. Cut grill and bumper from gray felt. Cut tires from black felt. To put together, do the following: On the turquoise base, put dots of glue around windshield edge and top edge of hood. Stretch plastic wrap over this area, pressing into glue. Put glue on top of plastic wrap around windshield and top hood area (glue will now be on both sides of plastic wrap). Place felt windshield piece over glue. (The plastic wrap should now be sandwiched between two pieces of felt on top of windshield.)

Glue the remaining felt pieces on in this order: fenders, grill, tires, bumpers, and lights. The front of the van should look like the pattern.

Glue the front of the van to the back of the van as indicated. DO NOT glue the windshield, for Oscar and Geraldene need to slip into the seat slits behind the windshield.

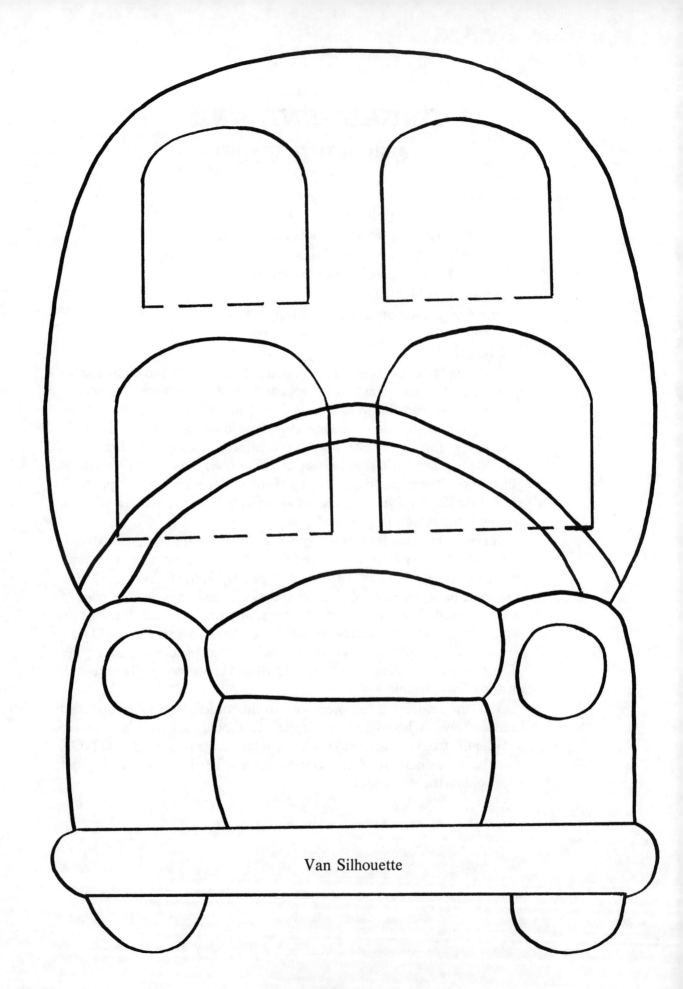

Van Silhouette

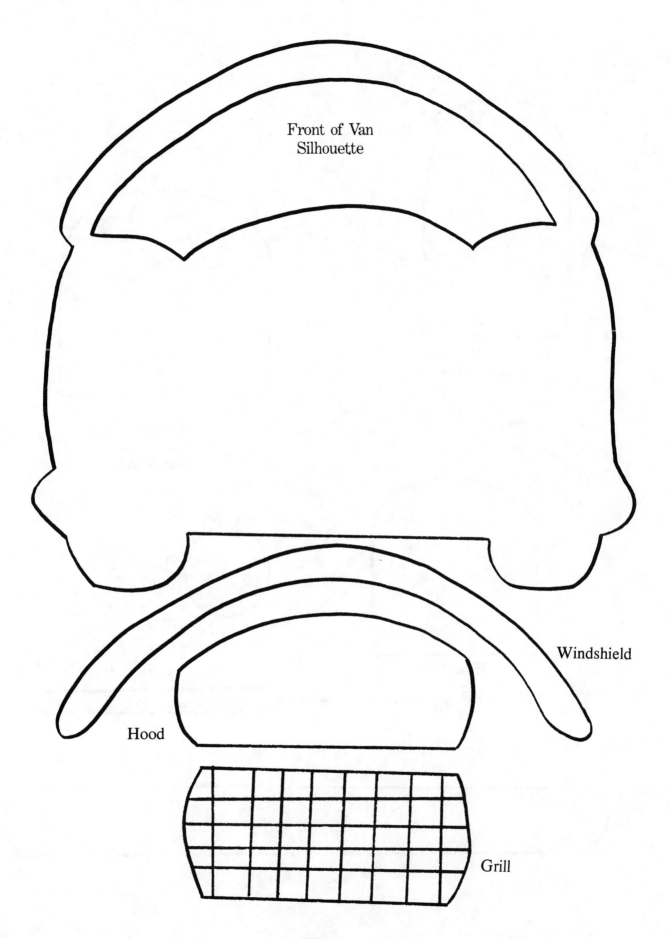

Front of Van
Silhouette

Windshield

Hood

Grill

69

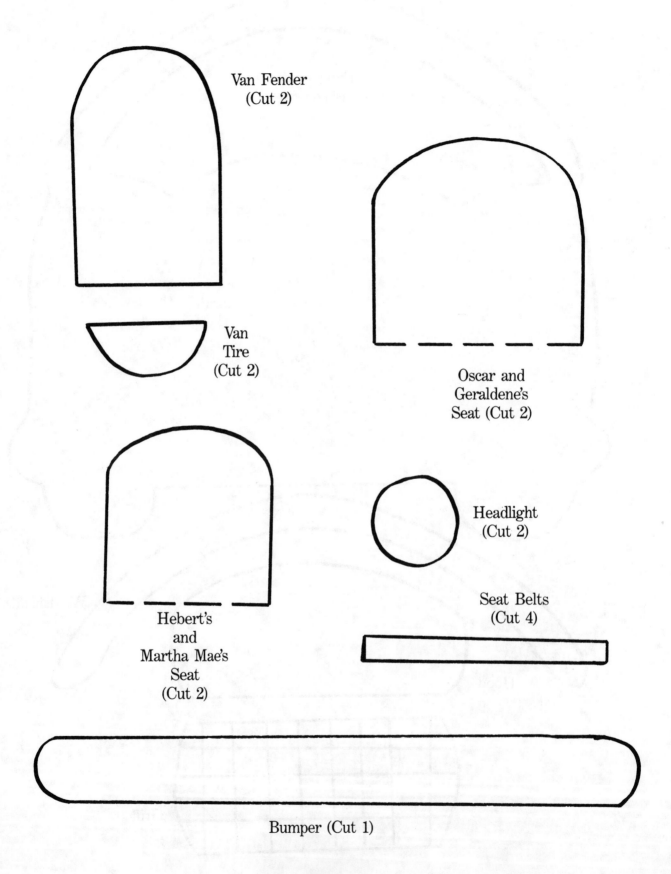

Van Fender
(Cut 2)

Van
Tire
(Cut 2)

Oscar and
Geraldene's
Seat (Cut 2)

Headlight
(Cut 2)

Seat Belts
(Cut 4)

Hebert's
and
Martha Mae's
Seat
(Cut 2)

Bumper (Cut 1)

CONTEMPORARY
STORIES

THE PINK PLASTIC PIG SISTERS' SPACE ADVENTURE

Storyteller: Over the hills and far away on a little farm lived the Pink Plastic Pig Sisters, Polly Esther and Polly Ethelene. Their home was a lovely muddy pig pen where they spent their days happily slipping and sliding around in the squishy mud. One day they saw the astronauts on TV flying all around in space in a space ship. Polly Esther said:

Polly Esther: "Oh, let's build a little space ship like that so we can fly all around in space."

Storyteller: And Polly Ethelene said:

Polly Ethelene: "And we could make little space suits and even little bubble hats like the astronauts."

Storyteller: So the Pink Plastic Pig Sisters got busy. They worked and worked on their space ship and their space suits. Finally, they were finished. They put on their space suits and their bubble hats. Polly Esther said:

Polly Esther: "Come on, Polly Ethelene, let's get in our little space ship so we can fly all around in space."

Storyteller: The Pink Plastic Pig Sisters climbed in the little space ship and fastened their seat belts. Polly Esther said:

Polly Esther: "Hold onto your hat because here we go . . . . . 10, 9, 8, 7, 6, 5, 4, 3, 2, 1, Blast Off!"

Storyteller: (With a loud hand clap) **BANG!** The little space ship shivered and shook and then it took off with a terrible roar. Polly Ethelene was scared to death of all that racket. She said:

Polly Ethelene: "Oink! Oink! Oink!"

Storyteller: Polly Esther said:

Polly Esther: "Hush, Girl. Quit that hollering, we gotta go fast to get up in space."

Storyteller: Polly Ethelene kept on hollering, though not so loud.

Polly Ethelene: "Oink! Oink! Oink!"

Storyteller: Away they went out into space. The little space ship went behind the moon, to the left of the sun and over the biggest star. And suddenly right in front of the pig sister was the rainbow.

Polly Ethelene: "Drive this little old space ship up close to the rainbow so we can see it good."

Storyteller: So Polly Esther drove right up to the rainbow. Polly Ethelene said:

Polly Ethelene: "I declare! That's the prettiest thing I ever did see! That rainbow's made out of jelly beans. Stop this thing and let me out."

Storyteller: So Polly Esther stopped the little space ship and Polly Ethelene climbed out onto the rainbow. That little old pig started eating jelly beans as fast as she could stuff them in her mouth. She said:

Polly Ethelene: "Slurp, slurp, slurp! This is hog heaven. I never saw so many jelly beans in my whole life."

Storyteller: Well, that greedy little pig was so busy eating jelly beans that she got up to the top of the rainbow before she knew it. All at once she started sliding down the other side. She said:

Polly Ethelene: "Oink! Oink! Oink! I'm falling off this rainbow. Do something, Polly Esther!"

Storyteller: Poor old Polly Ethelene slid almost off the rainbow, but she held on for dear life, just hanging there over space.

Polly Esther: "Hold on, girl! I'm coming to the rescue!"

Storyteller: So Polly Esther drove the little space ship right above poor Polly Ethelene and dropped a rope down to her.

Storyteller: Well, Polly Esther pulled and pulled on the rope. Finally she got Polly Ethelene up to the door of the little space ship. But! There was a terrible problem! That Polly Ethelene had eaten so many rainbow jelly beans that she was too fat to get in the door of the little space ship.

Polly Esther pulled and pulled on the rope, but Polly Ethelene would not come in the door. Polly Ethelene said:

Polly Ethelene: "Oink! Oink! Oink! Quit pulling on me! You're about to squeeze me in two."

Storyteller: Polly Esther said:

Polly Esther: Well, you just acted like a pig and ate too many jelly beans. Now look at you. You're fat as a blimp! I can't get you in the door so I guess I'll just have to pull you by the rope back to our little farm."

Storyteller: And that's just what she did. That poor old Polly Ethelene did look just like a blimp on a rope. She said:

Polly Ethelene: "Oink! Oink! Oink!"

Storyteller: That poor little pig cried and shivered and shook all the way back home.

After the Pink Plastic Pig Sisters were safely back in their pig pen, Polly Ethelene said:

Polly Ethelene: "You won't ever get me back in that space ship again. I'm through with flying around in space. I'm going to stay right here in this squishy, sloshy mud from now on. But those sure were good jelly beans! Smack! Smack!"

THE MAGIC MACHINE

Storyteller: If you should look up into the sky on a dark night, you may see many stars. On one of these stars lives a group of people called the Starlettes. They are very small and they are in the shape of stars. They love to sing, dance, and play, but most of all they love to learn new things.

One day a very special box fell from the sky and everyone ran to see what it might be. Sammy Starlette was the first to get to the box.

Sammy: (In an excited voice) "Oh, what could be in the box!"

Stella: "Why don't we open the box and see what is inside? There are some words on the box and it says, 'COMPUTER, HANDLE WITH CARE'."

Storyteller: All of the Starlettes knew that if you handle something with care, it means to be soft and tender, but they did not know what the other strange word "computer" could mean. Because Starlettes love to learn new things, they started to open the big box to see just what this magic machine could be. They slowly untied the big red bow that held the box together and suddenly the box fell open.

Susie: "Look, it must be a television. It has a big screen and a cord that you would plug into a wall for electricity."

Steve: "I think it is a typewriter. It has little buttons that have all the letters of the alphabet and numbers too."

Sammy: "I do not think that this is a television or a typewriter. It has too many buttons to be a television and it has these little records that fit in this hole on the side." (Insert record into slot on side of computer character.)

Stella: "I do not think that this is a typewriter because it has many different letters that I have never seen before."

Sammy: "I have found a book in the box that tells all about this computer. If I read the book, I can learn how to turn on this magic machine."

Starlettes: "Yeah, Yeah, Yeah! Turn on the computer. Turn on the computer."

Storyteller: By this time almost every Starlette was in the middle of town watching Sammy learn how to turn on the magic machine. Suddenly a strange bleep came from the computer and the word 'hello' was on the screen.

Computer: (In a robot voice) "Hello, I am a computer. I can help you learn so many new things.

Steve: "Can we learn to add and subtract numbers?"

Computer: "Yes, we can add 123456789 and 987654321 and get the right answer fast!"

Stella: "Can we learn to write letters and stories?"

Computer: "Yes, we can write anything we want to write and everyone will be able to learn new things. I have records that can teach you how to use my buttons so that you can do all of these things."

Storyteller: All of the Starlettes were so happy to have the friendly computer. Everyone took turns in reading the book and learning how to use the magic machine.

THE RACCOON COUSINS' ROCK-N-ROLL BAND

Storyteller: The five raccoon girl cousins who lived in Coon Holler decided that they would start an all-girls rock-n-roll band. They met under the old oak tree by Crooked Creek to make their plans for the Coon Holler Rainbow Rock-N-Roll Band.

Minnie, the oldest cousin, liked to sew and make clothes for herself. She said:

Minnie: "I can design and make our costumes for our Rock-N-Roll Band."

Storyteller: Everyone agreed that Minnie could do this very well.

May Belle, the next oldest, sang and played the guitar at school, the church socials, and at family get-togethers. She said:

May Belle: "I can choose the songs we'll sing and write the harmony for our Rock-N-Roll Band."

Storyteller: The girl cousins thought this was a great idea for they really liked to hear May Belle sing. Myrtle, the next oldest cousin, was good at drawing. She drew posters for special meetings in Coon Holler. The girl cousins asked her to design posters for their Coon Holler Rainbow Rock-N-Roll Band. Myrtle said:

Myrtle: "Oh, I do like to draw and will have fun making our posters."

Storyteller: Mattie, the next to youngest of the girl cousins, was a tomboy. She liked to work on machines, especially Uncle Jasper's old pick-up truck. She said:

Mattie: "We'll need a van to travel around in. I can get one from Mr. Bob and paint a big, beautiful rainbow on the side so everyone will know who we are."

Storyteller: Everyone agreed that this was a wonderful idea.

When the girl cousins got to Missy, the youngest, they couldn't think of anything she could do. They finally decided that she could help Minnie make the costumes. The next day, Missy went to help Minnie make the costumes, but when Missy tried to put the pattern on the material, it tore in half. Minnie got so upset she said:

Minnie: "Missy, go away. You can't help me, you're too little and clumsy."

Storyteller: Missy went outside and cried and cried.

That night when the cousins met beneath the old oak tree by Crooked Creek in Coon Holler, Minnie told them what happened. Missy looked very sad and had big tears in her eyes. Everyone felt sorry for her and decided that she could help May Belle copy the music for the Rock-N-Roll Band.

The next morning, Missy went to May Belle's house to help copy the music. May Belle had the paper, pen and ink ready for them to work. Missy crawled up in the chair and reached for a pen to write with. When she did this, she knocked the ink over and it spilled all over May Belle's music. May Belle got so upset she shouted:

May Belle: "Go away, Missy. You just can't help me. Look what you've done. You ruined the music. You're just too little and clumsy to help."

Storyteller: Missy ran out the door and cried and cried.

That night when the cousins met under the old oak tree by Crooked Creek in Coon Holler, May Belle told them about the disaster with the music. Poor Missy looked so sad with tears in her eyes. Myrtle said:

Myrtle: "Surely Missy can help me hang our posters about our concerts. I can't think how she could make a mess of them."

Storyteller: So, it was agreed that Missy could help Myrtle.

The next morning Missy met Myrtle by the blackberry patch in Coon Holler. Myrtle gave Missy the can of nails to carry. As they walked down the path to hang up the posters, Missy stumped her toe on a rock and fell down. The nails flew everywhere. They rolled under rocks and bushes. Myrtle and Missy looked everywhere for them, but they were nowhere to be found. Myrtle was furious. She said:

Myrtle: "Everyone is right. You are too clumsy and too little to do anything."

Storyteller: Missy cried and cried all the way home.

That night in Coon Holler beneath the old oak tree by Crooked Creek, the girl cousins shook their heads when they heard what had happened. They wanted to tell Missy she couldn't be in their band but she looked so sad. They decided to give her another chance. She could help Mattie paint the van. Missy said:

Missy: "Oh, I'll try hard to help and not make a mess of things."

Storyteller: The next morning Missy went to help Mattie paint the rainbow on the van. She had on her raggedy clothes so she would not ruin her good clothes. Mattie gave her the yellow paint and a brush to begin painting. She did fine for a while and was feeling happy. She came to a point that she couldn't reach. Missy put down the brush and went to get a big rock to stand on. She got the rock right where she wanted it, picked up the brush and climbed up on the rock. She reached up to paint and would you believe she lost her balance and fell off that rock right into the can of yellow paint.

When Mattie came to see what all the commotion was about she shouted and screamed:

Mattie: "Everyone is right. You are too little and clumsy to do anything."

Storyteller: Missy went home and her mother scrubbed all the yellow paint off her and rocked her in the big rocking chair. Missy cried and said:

Missy: "Momma, why can't I do anything right?"

Momma: "Why baby, you can do something. Everyone can. You just have to find what you do best."

Storyteller: The next day Missy thought and thought about what she could do best. She went for a walk in Coon Holler. She picked up a stick while she was walking. She passed a big rock and took that stick and beat on it. Rum-Da-Dum Dum. When she passed the old tree stump she took her stick and played boom-da-boom-da on it.

Missy thought so hard. She said to herself:

Missy: "All I can do is play rum-da-dum-dum on rocks and boom-da-boom-da on old tree stumps."

Storyteller: Then a thought came to her. She ran home and got out momma's big wash tub and the old broken butter churn. She took her stick and began to beat beautiful rhythms on them.

Storyteller: The girl cousins heard this wonderful sound and went to see what it was.

They were suprised when they saw Missy making such wonderful rhythms. Then a thought came to them. They ran to Missy and said:

All: "Missy, you can do something. You can play the drums in our Rock-N-Roll Band."

Storyteller: Missy was so happy. She found what she could do and if you ever go to Coon Holler, be sure to go to hear Missy in the Coon Holler Rainbow Rock-N-Roll Band.

THE PINK PLASTIC PIG SISTERS'
SPACE ADVENTURE
SISTERS

MATERIALS:
- One 9 X 12 inch piece pink felt
- One 5 X 6 inch piece blue, yellow, and light green felt
- Scraps of raspberry and white felt
- Two pair 8mm wiggle eyes
- Ribbon
- Star sequins
- Permanent black marking pens

DIRECTIONS:

Using pattern, cut two pig silhouettes and noses from pink felt. Cut cheeks from raspberry felt.

Glue eyes, nose, and cheeks in place.

Draw nose marks and mouth with black marking pen.

POLLY ESTHER

Cut overalls from blue felt, blouse from calico print, and collar from white felt.

Put together in this order: blouse, overalls, and collar.

Make a bow from ribbon and attach to one of the pig's ears.

POLLY ETHELENE

Using pattern, cut pants, buttons, and collar from green felt. Cut blouse from yellow felt.

Put together in the following order: blouse, buttons, collar, and pants.

Glue a star sequin next to one of pig's ears.

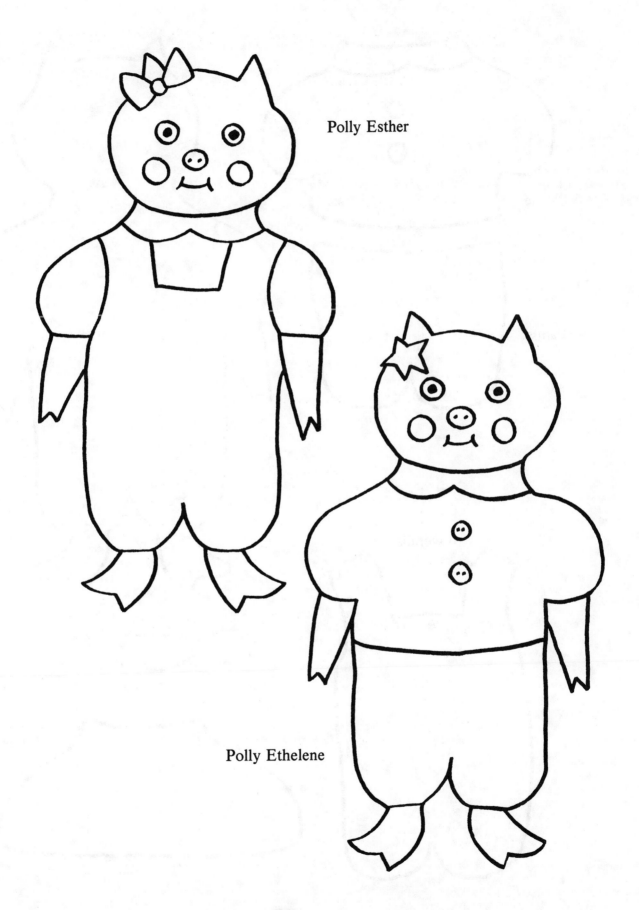

Polly Esther

Polly Ethelene

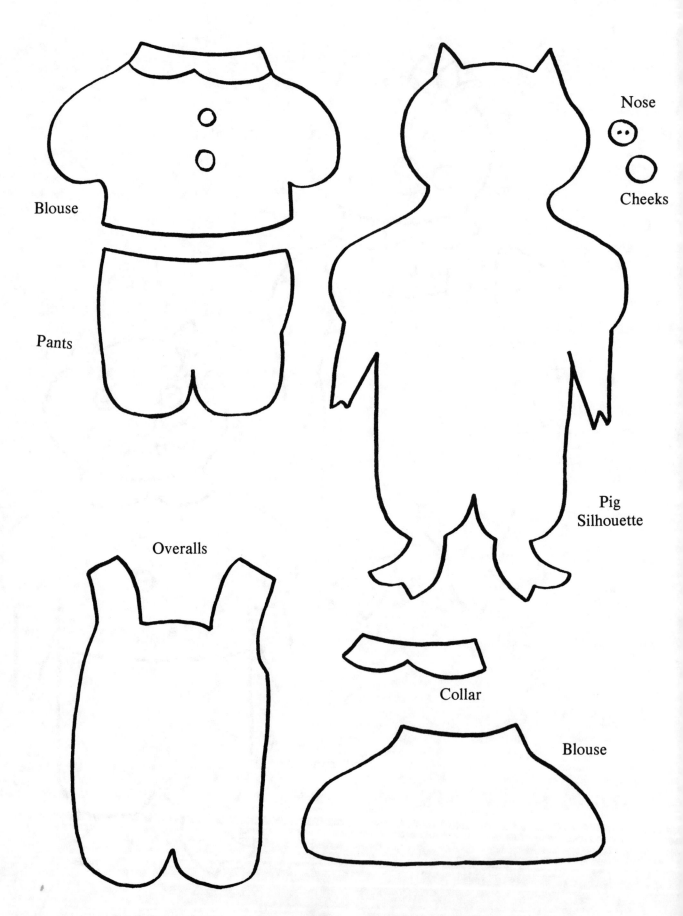

Blouse

Pants

Nose

Cheeks

Pig
Silhouette

Overalls

Collar

Blouse

80

SPACE SUIT

MATERIALS:
—One 9 X 12 inch piece gray felt
—Two 4 X 6 inch pieces aluminum foil
—Two 3-inch squares plastic wrap or cellophane

DIRECTIONS:
Using pattern, cut two space suit shapes from gray felt. Cut two space suit shapes from aluminum foil. Cut out face area indicated on pattern.

Put dots of glue around helmet edge of felt space suit. Stretch plastic wrap over this area and press into glue.

Put dots of glue around edge of entire space suit, including helmet.

Place aluminum foil space suit over felt space suit and press into glue. When suit has dried 24 hours, trim excess plastic wrap away from helmet.

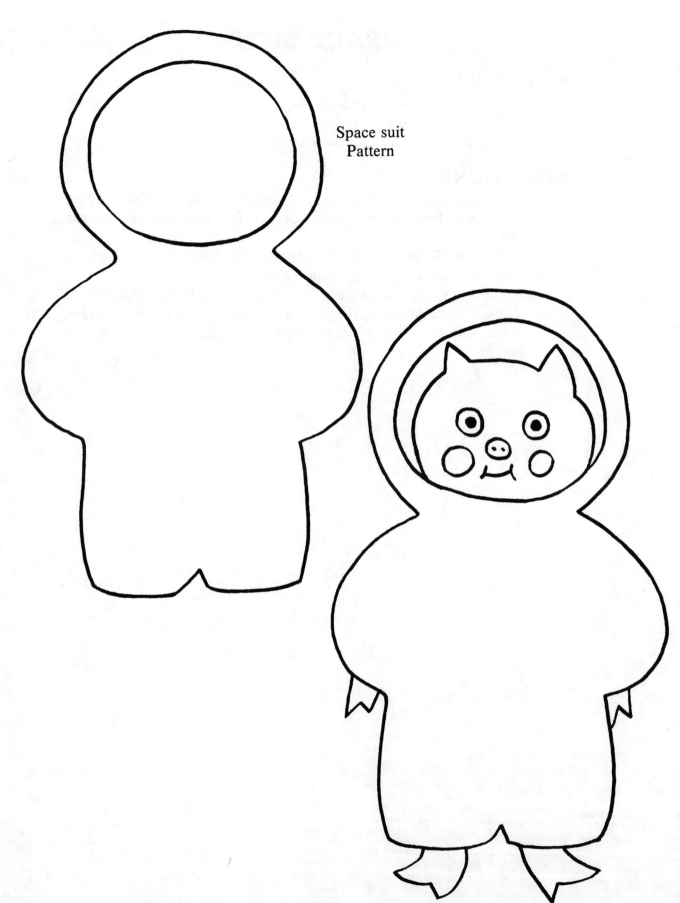

Space suit
Pattern

82

FAT PIG IN SPACE SUIT

MATERIALS:
- —One 9 X 12 inch piece gray felt
- —One 9 X 4 inch piece aluminum foil
- —One 3-inch square of plastic wrap or cellophane
- —Scraps of pink and raspberry felt
- —One pair 5mm wiggle eyes
- —Small amount of polyester fiberfill
- —Needle and pink thread
- —Permanent black marking pen

DIRECTIONS:

Using pattern, cut two spacesuit shapes from the gray felt and one from aluminum foil. Cut face area out of ONE felt suit and the aluminum foil suit. The solid gray shape will serve as the base for constructing this figure.

Cut two feet, two hands, and fat pig face from pink felt. Cut two fat cheeks from raspberry felt. Put fat pig in spacesuit together as follows:

Head: Take two pinches of polyester fiberfill and place under raspberry cheeks. Using needle and thread, stitch cheeks into place on the head using small running stitches. (Use needle to stuff the fiberfill under the cheeks as you stitch them in place.) Glue nose and eyes into place. With marker, make nose marks and wrinkles in chin. Glue star sequin to one of pig's ears.

Glue head to solid helmet of felt space suit so that it will show through front of helmet. Glue hands and feet to ends of arms and legs of the solid felt suit. Put a wad of fiberfill in stomach area and place second felt suit on top. With needle and thread, sew around stomach area through both layers of suits. This will make stomach pouchy in front. Put glue between felt suits and press together.

Add plastic wrap and aluminum foil suit in the same manner as described in the directions for the space suits.

Use a piece of heavy gray yarn for the tether between the space ship and the fat pig in her space suit.

Fat
Pig

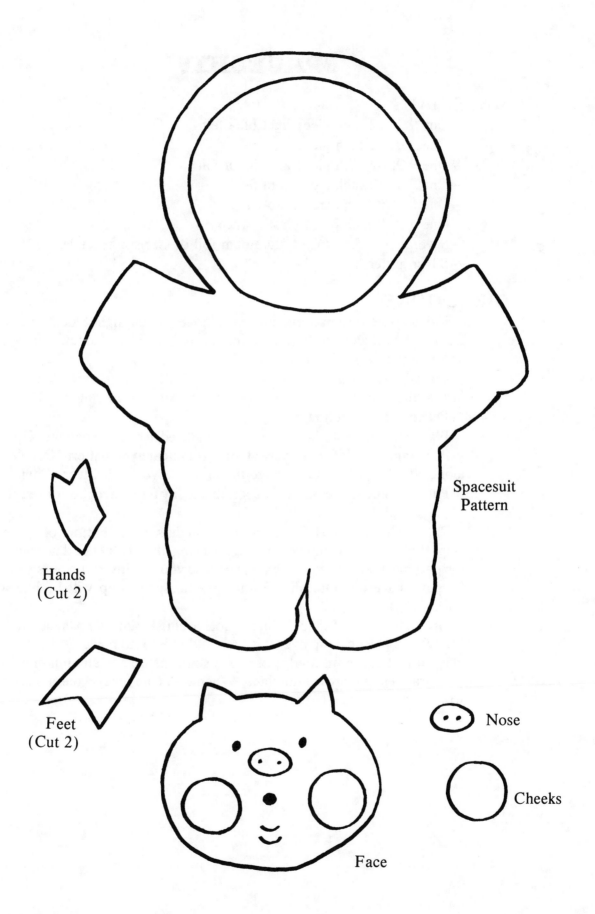

Spacesuit
Pattern

Hands
(Cut 2)

Feet
(Cut 2)

Nose

Cheeks

Face

SPACESHIP

MATERIALS:
- —One 9 X 12 inch piece light blue felt
- —One 9 X 12 inch piece gray felt
- —One 9 X 12 inch piece aluminum foil
- —One 9 X 12 inch piece gold felt
- —One 5 X 6 inch piece yellow felt
- —One 5 X 9 inch piece plastic wrap
- —Several ¼-inch strips of aluminum foil or Christmas icicles
- —Silver glitter

DIRECTIONS:

Using space ship pattern, cut one silhouette from light blue felt, one from gray felt, and one from aluminum foil. The light blue felt ship will serve as the back of space ship.

Cut windshield area out of gray felt and aluminum space ship. Cut largest flame from orange felt and smaller flame from yellow felt.

Put together as follows:

Place aluminum strips along upper middle edge of orange flame. Glue yellow flame to middle of orange flame as indicated on pattern. Put glue along edge of yellow and orange flame and cover with silver glitter.

Put light blue shape on working arera and lay flame over bottom edge. Glue into place.

Put dots of glue over flame and up straight sides of bottom of space ship. Place gray felt ship on top and press together. (NOTE: The round top part must not be glued to back, because you will insert the pig sisters in their spacesuits into ship from top—the space ship will be like a pocket.)

On outside edge of space ship, put dots of glue around windshield area. Stretch the plastic wrap over this area and press into place. Put dots of glue around entire front edge of space ship, then place aluminum ship over gray felt and press into place. When dry, trim away excess plastic wrap from windshield.

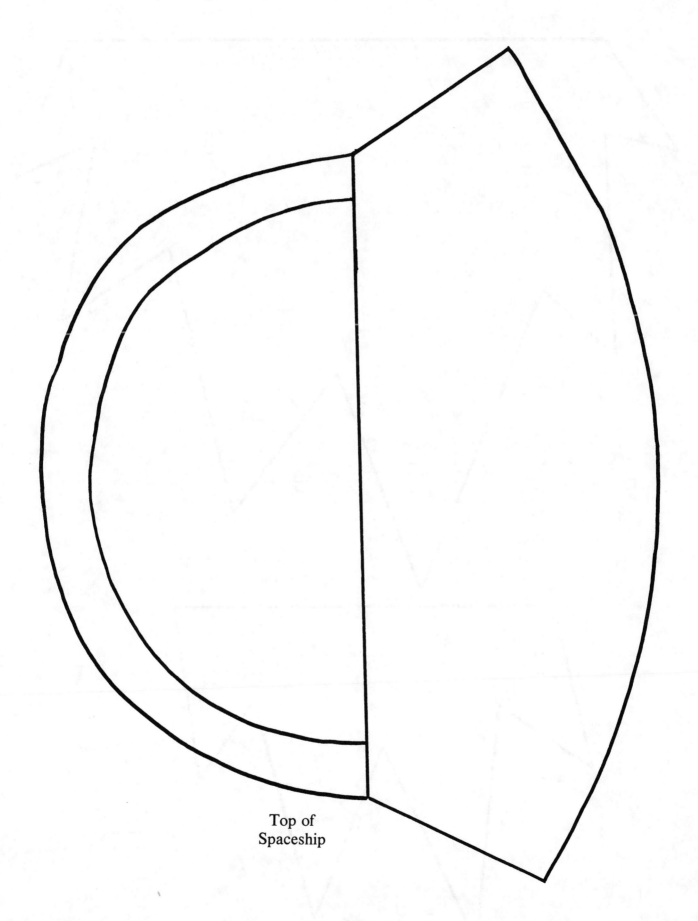

Top of
Spaceship

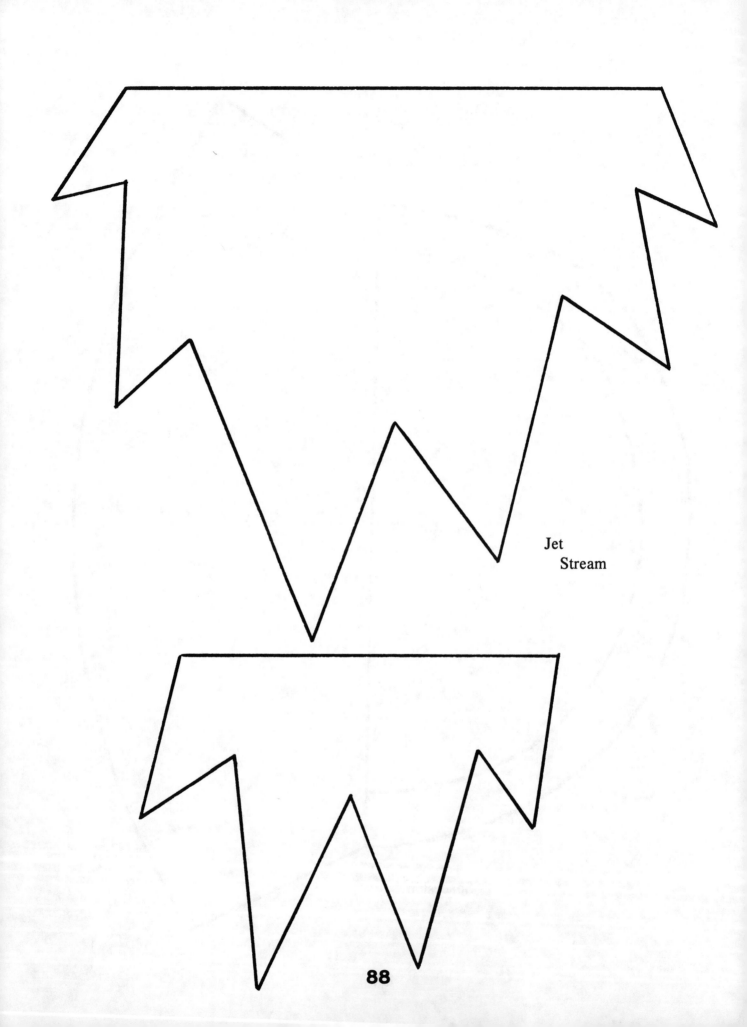

Jet
Stream

88

JELLY BEAN RAINBOW

MATERIALS:

—One 9 X 24 inch piece of red, orange, yellow, green, and blue felt

DIRECTIONS:

Using pattern, put whole rainbow on folded red felt and cut base for rainbow.

Cut one stripe of each of the five colors (be sure to place pattern on fold or you will have just half a rainbow.)

Glue strips to red base.

Cut out jelly bean shapes from the five rainbow colors. You will need 16 red, 14 orange, 12 yellow, 10 green, and 8 blue.

Glue eight red jelly beans to the upper right-hand side of the rainbow. Eight are not glued to the left, so that the teacher can take them off as the pig eats them. Glue the jelly beans on the rest of the rainbow.

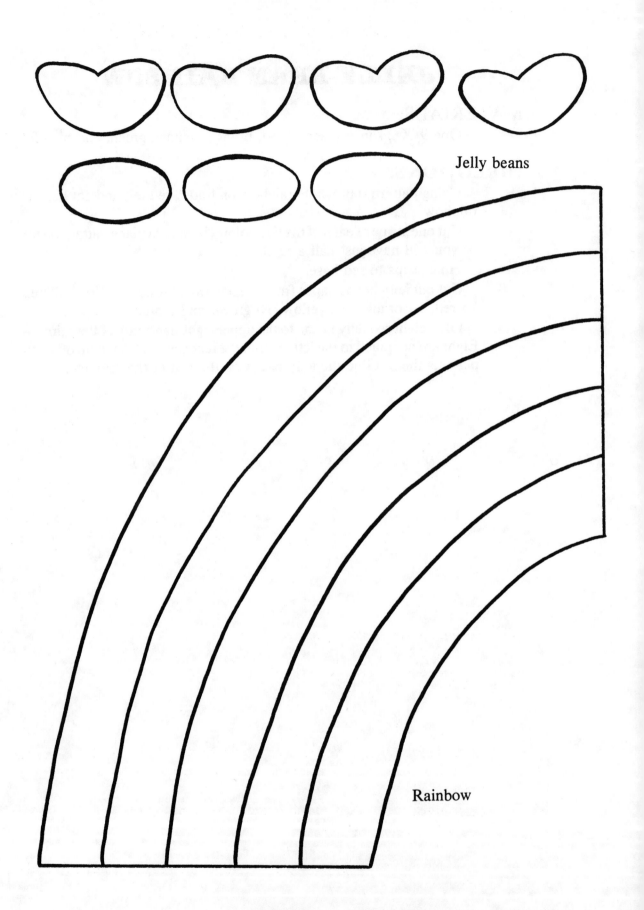

Jelly beans

Rainbow

THE MAGIC MACHINE
COMPUTER

MATERIALS:
—4 X 9 inch piece gray felt
—4 X 9 inch piece light blue felt
—Two 5mm wiggle eyes
—One 3-inch square plastic wrap or cellophane
—One 1-inch square poster board
—Scraps black felt
—Permanent black marking pen

DIRECTIONS:
Using patterns, cut one computer silhouette from light blue felt for base. Cut three computer parts from gray felt. Cut slot in disk drive with fingernail scissors. Cut screen area out of monitor so blue of base will show through.

Put together as follows:

On light blue base, glue wiggle eyes and draw mouth as indicated on the pattern. Put dots of glue around the upper edge of the blue base. Stretch plastic wrap over this area to make screen for the monitor. Glue middle piece of computer on next. Glue screen over plastic wrap, then glue the keyboard onto bottom. Glue keys onto the keyboard and switch onto the disk drive as indicated on the pattern.

The 1-inch piece of poster board will serve as the floppy disk that can be inserted in the slot of the disk drive.

PACKAGE

MATERIALS:
—One 9 X 12 piece gray felt
—One 9 X 12 piece aluminum foil
—One bow made from ½-inch ribbon
—Permanent black marking pen

DIRECTIONS:
Using pattern, cut box silhouette from felt and aluminum foil. Put dots of glue along edges of felt and place aluminum foil over top and press into place.

With black marker, make markings on package as indicated on the pattern.

Glue bow on top of package.

Place package over computer before you begin telling the story to the children.

Package

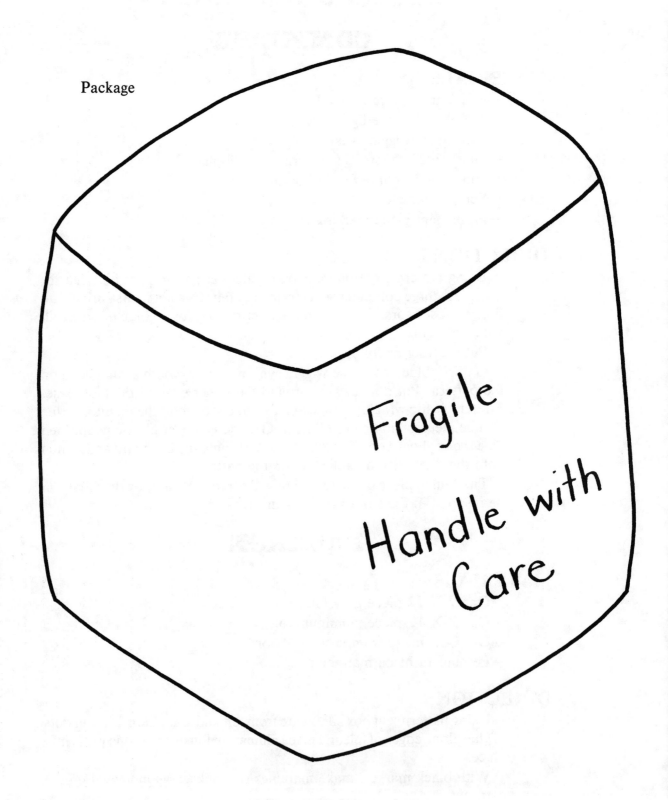

Fragile

Handle with Care

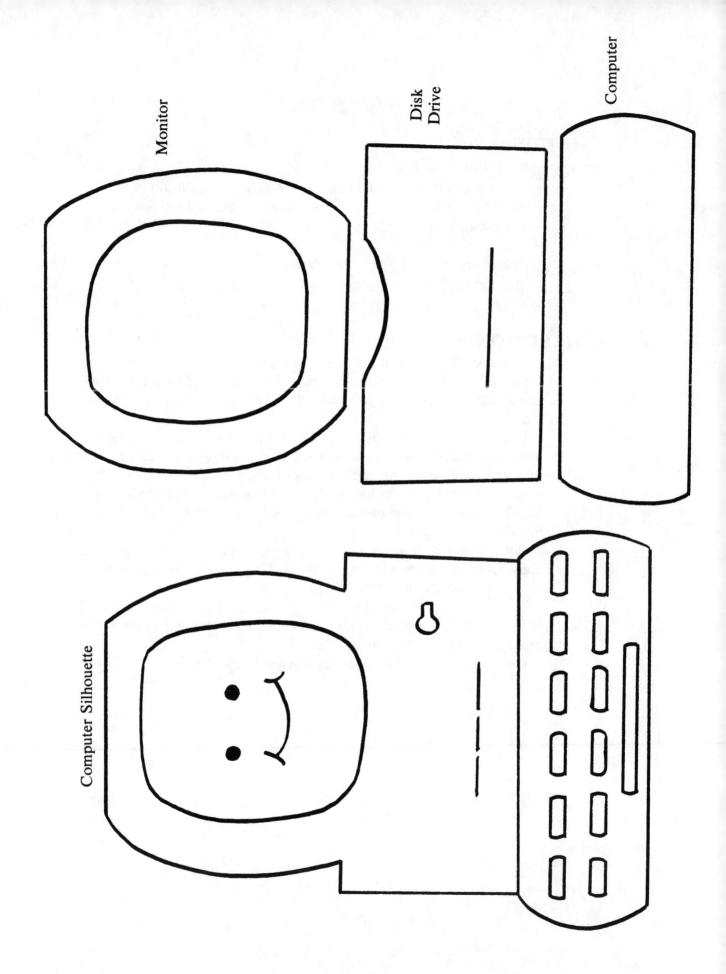

Monitor

Disk
Drive

Computer

Computer Silhouette

STARS

MATERIALS:

- —¼ yard of white felt
- —5 X 9 inch pieces of bright green, magenta, gold, turquoise felt
- —Scraps of dark green, light yellow, blue, black, and red felt
- —Three pair 8mm wiggle eyes
- —¼-inch wide ribbon
- —Rhinestones
- —Silver glitter
- —Feathers

DIRECTIONS:

There are four stars in the story, two boys and two girls. Make two silhouettes with right hand going up and two with right hand pointing down. Think "bright" as you cut their clothes (star shape), arms, and legs.

Using the patterns, cut four silhouettes from the white felt. When the parts are glued on, it will appear that the stars are standing on clouds. Cut four star bodies from the bright colors of felt. Cut their hands and legs from a complementary color of felt. Cut three pair of star-shaped eyes from black felt. Cut one pair of star-shaped glasses from black felt. Cut mouths from red felt.

Put together as follows: On white base, place arms and legs, then body. Glue into place. On three of the bodies, glue star eyes and wiggle eyes. Glue mouth into place.

For fourth star, make the star-shaped glasses from black felt and outline with silver glitter. Glue rhinestones on the star's wrists for bracelets. Glue feathers in her "hair."

On the other girl, glue a bow or flowers in her "hair."

Star (Make 4)

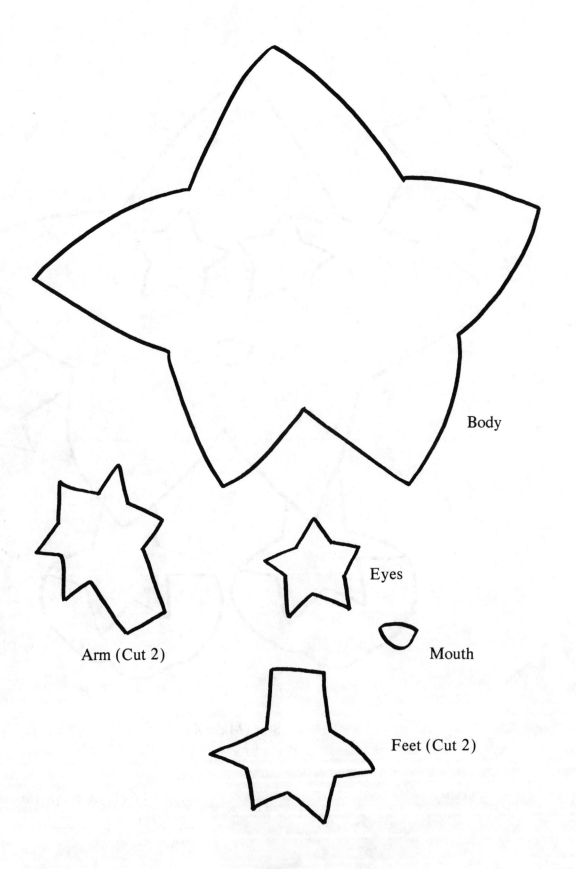

Body

Arm (Cut 2)

Eyes

Mouth

Feet (Cut 2)

THE RACCOON COUSINS'
ROCK-N-ROLL BAND

This story is made on the non-woven interfacing. Instructions for making figures on non-woven interfacing can be found preceding the Winky Witch story.

Brush

Can

Mary
Belle

Mattie

Stick

Churn

Myrtle

Stump

Minnie

98

Pan

NAILS

Missie

Rainbow
Rock-N-Roll
Band

Rock

Costume

99

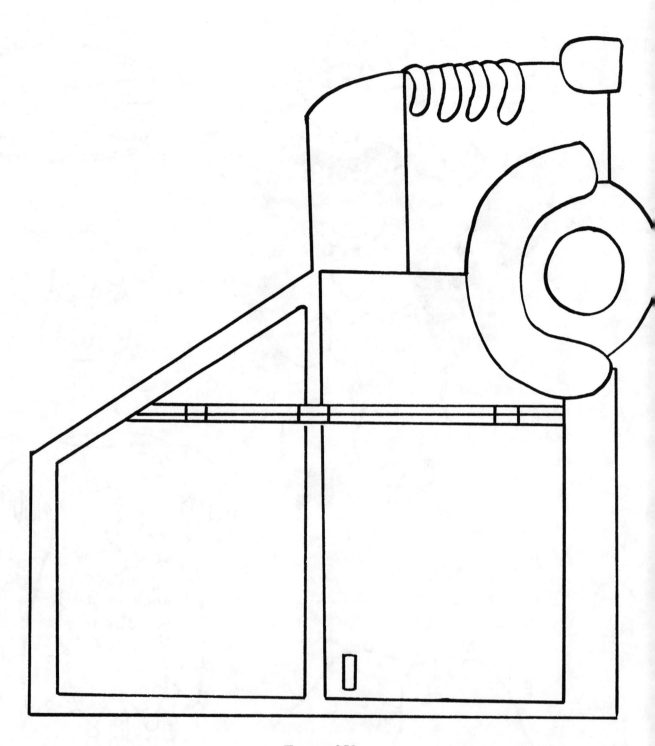

Front of Van

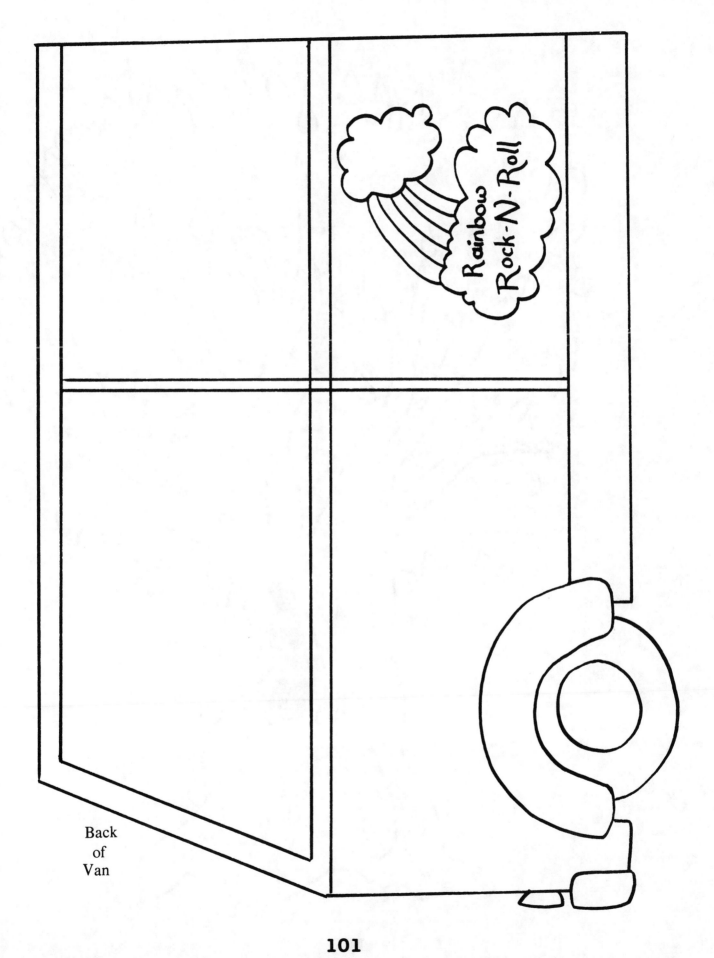

Back
of
Van

Rainbow Rock-N-Roll

Tree

TRADITIONAL STORIES

NOAH'S ARK

This flannel board story is different from the others in this book in that it is to be recorded on a cassette tape and played as you put the flannel board figures on the flannel board. This method is especially good to use if the story has a lot of rhyming words or hard to remember phrases. It is also a good way to let the children hear another voice, particularly a male voice, if the children are around female voices most of the day.

Storyteller: God said, "Noah you better listen to my word. The people are acting awful and I'm going to send a flood.

Gather up your family and the animals two by two. Build yourself a boat big enough to hold a zoo.

Noah called his sons Shem, Ham, and Japeth to help him with this chore. Their wives and Mrs. Noah gathered food and clothes by the score.

Noah listened carefully and worked from morn 'til dark. When he finished his hammering he had a mighty fine ark.

Noah's sons helped him gather the animals as directed. Two of every kind of beast from the biggest to the smallest was selected.

The elephants lumbered along the way. The giraffe came eating fresh, green hay.

The kangaroos hopped, thumping their feet. The tigers growled hoping there was fresh meat.

The humble mice chattered away, hoping to find a warm, dry place to stay.

When all the animals and Noah's family got on board, God closed the ark and started the flood.

The rain fell forty days and forty nights. Water was everywhere in sight.

After a while, it's a fact, the ark stopped on top of Mount Ararat.

Noah sent out a dove, dry land to seek. The dove returned with an olive twig in its beak.

The earth was dry again, ready for new life,

Noah left the ark with his family and his wife.

God loved Noah's family and a promise he did share,

A rainbow in the sky is a sign that God really cares.

A covenant, God said, I make with you, please trust my word,

The earth will never again be totally destroyed by a flood.

Noah listened fully and followed God's word.

A kind, gentle honest man by God was truly loved.

THE THREE
BILLY GOATS GRUFF

Storyteller: Once upon a time there were three billy goats. There was a little tiny baby billy goat. And there was a middle-sized billy goat. And there was a great big billy goat. These billy goats had eaten all the green grass on their hill. The little tiny baby billy goat said in his little tiny voice:

Baby Billy Goat: "All of our green grass is eaten up and I am hungry."

Storyteller: The middle-sized billy goat said, in his middle-sized voice:

Middle-sized Billy Goat: "I am hungry, too. Whatever will we do?"

Storyteller: The great big billy goat said, in his great big voice:

Great Big Billy Goat: "Look, over across the river there is another hill of green grass. Let's go over the river on the bridge to the other hill so we can eat green grass and grow fat."

Storyteller: Well, the billy goats did not know that a troll lived under the bridge. This troll was very mean. Whenever anyone tried to cross his bridge he ate them up. He especially liked to eat billy goats. The little tiny baby billy goat started across the bridge. He went "trip-trap, trip-trap" over the bridge. The mean old troll came out from under the bridge and he said:

Troll: "Stop, billy goat. This is my bridge and I eat up people who cross my bridge. I am going to eat you."

Storyteller: The little tiny baby billy goat said in his little tiny voice:

Baby Billy Goat: "Oh, please, Mr. Troll, don't eat me up. I am just a little tiny baby billy goat. My brother, the middle-sized billy goat, is going to cross your bridge. He is much bigger than I am and he would be a nice dinner for you."

Storyteller: And the mean old troll said:

Troll: "Very well, baby billy goat, you can cross my bridge. I will wait for the middle-sized billy goat and eat him up."

Storyteller: So the little tiny baby billy goat went on across the bridge, "trip-trap, trip-trap." The middle-sized billy goat started across the bridge. He went "trip-trap, trip-trap" over the bridge. The mean old troll said:

Troll: "Stop, billy goat. This is my bridge and I eat people who cross my bridge. I am going to eat you up."

Storyteller: The middle-sized billy goat said, in his middle-sized voice:

Middle-sized Bill Goat: "Oh, please, Mr. Troll, I am just a middle-sized billy goat. My brother, the great big billy goat, is going to cross your bridge. He is much bigger than I am and he would be a nice dinner for you."

Storyteller: And the mean old troll said:

Troll: "Very well, middle-sized billy goat, you can cross my bridge. I will wait for the great big billy goat and eat him up."

Storyteller: So the middle-sized billy goat went on across the bridge "TRIP-TRAP, TRIP-TRAP."

The great big billy goat started across the bridge. He went "TRIP-TRAP, TRIP-TRAP" over the bridge. The mean old troll said:

Troll: "Stop, billy goat. This is my bridge and I eat people who cross my bridge. I let your two brothers go on across, but I am going to eat you up. I am very hungry now and you'll be just the right size for my dinner."

Storyteller: The great big billy goat said in his great big voice:

Great Big Billy Goat: "Oh, no you won't eat ME, Mr. Troll!!"

Storyteller: And with that the great big billy goat butted the troll off the bridge and into the river and he was never seen again. The great big billy goat went on across the bridge, "TRIP-TRAP, TRIP-TRAP." He and his brothers lived happily ever after on the hill where they ate green grass and grew fat.

    Snip, snap, snout
    This tale's told out.

THREE LITTLE PIGS

Storyteller: Once upon a time there were three little pigs who lived in a house with their mama. One day the mama pig said:

Mama Pig: "Children, you are all grown up now and it is time for you to go out in the world and live in your own little houses."

Storyteller: So the little pigs left their mama and went out in to the world to build their own little houses. The first little pig met a man carrying a load of straw and he said:

First Pig: "Please, man, will you give me some of your straw to build myself a little house?"

Storyteller: The man gave the little pig some of his straw and he built a nice little straw house for himself.

The second little pig met a man carrying a load of sticks. He said:

Second Pig: "Please, man, will you give me some of your sticks to build myself a little house?"

Storyteller: The man gave the little pig some of his sticks and he built a nice little stick house for himself.

The third little pig met a man carrying a load of bricks and he said:

Third Pig: "Please, man, will you give me some of your bricks to build myself a little house?"

Storyteller: The man gave the little pig some of his bricks and he built a nice little brick house for himself.

I wish I could tell you that the three little pigs lived happily ever after in their little houses . . . but in the woods where the little pigs built their houses, there lived a big bad wolf. The big bad wolf was always hungry and little pigs were his favorite things to eat.

The big bad wolf heard that three little pigs had built their houses in his woods so one day when he was hungry he went out to find them. He came to the first little pig's house which was made out of straw and he said:

Wolf: "Little pig, little pig, let me come in."

Storyteller: The little pig was afraid of the big bad wolf and he said:

First Pig: "No, no, by the hair of my chinny-chin-chin, I won't let you come in."

Storyteller: And the big bad wolf said:

Wolf: "Then I'll huff and I'll puff and I'll blow your house in."

Storyteller: And that's just what he did. He huffed and he puffed and he blew the house in and ate up the little pig.

Then the wolf went on down the road and he came to the second little pig's house which was made out of sticks. He said:

Wolf: "Little pig, little pig, let me come in."

Storyteller: The little pig was afraid of the big bad wolf and he said:

Second Pig: "No, no, by the hair on my chinny-chin-chin, I won't let you come in."

Storyteller: And the big bad wolf said:

Wolf: "Then I'll huff and I'll puff and I'll blow your house in."

Storyteller: And that's just what he did. He huffed and he puffed and he blew the house in and ate up the little pig.

Then the wolf went on down the road and he came to the third little pig's house which was made out of bricks. He said:

Wolf: "Little pig, little pig, let me come in."

Storyteller: The little pig said:

Third pig: "No, no, by the hair on my chinny-chin-chin, I won't let you come in."

Storyteller: And the big bad wolf said:

Wolf: "Then I'll huff and I'll puff and I'll blow your house in."

Storyteller: The big bad wolf huffed and he puffed, but he couldn't blow the house in because it was made of bricks. The wolf got really mad and he huffed and he puffed and he said:

Wolf: "Little pig, I am hungry and I am going to get in your house and eat you up. I'll just climb up on your house and come down the chimney!"

Storyteller: Well, this little pig was a smart little pig. He got his biggest pot and filled it with water. Then he put it on his fire until it was boiling hot. Finally, the big bad wolf climbed up on the little pig's roof. He said:

Wolf: "Little pig, here I come to eat you up."

Storyteller: And the big bad wolf jumped in the chimney and fell right into the big pot of boiling water. And that was the end of the big bad wolf. The little pig lived happily ever after in his little brick house.

THE GINGERBREAD BOY

Storyteller: Once upon a time there was a little old woman and a little old man who had no children. The Little Old Woman said:

Old Woman: "Sakes alive! It's lonely around here with no children."

Storyteller: So she decided to make a Gingerbread Boy to surprise the little old man. She made a fine Gingerbread Boy with raisins for his eyes and a cherry for his mouth. She popped him into the oven to bake. After awhile she opened the oven to see if he was finished. That Gingerbread Boy jumped right out of the oven and started to run away. The Little Old Woman said:

Old Woman: "Stop, stop, Gingerbread Boy."

Storyteller: But the Gingerbread Boy ran out the door saying:

Gingerbread Boy: "Run, run as fast as you can. You can't catch me. I'm the Gingerbread Man."

Storyteller: And run away he did! But the Little Old Woman ran after him.
The Gingerbread Boy ran on until he met a dog. The dog said:

Dog: "Stop, stop, Gingerbread Boy I am hungry and I want to eat you up."

Storyteller: "But the Gingerbread Boy Ran on, saying:

Gingerbread Boy: "Run, run as fast as you can. You can't catch me. I'm the Gingerbread Man."

Storyteller:And run away he did! But the dog ran after the Little Old Woman who was running after the Gingerbread Boy.
The Gingerbread Boy ran on until he met a cat. The cat said:

Cat: "Stop, stop, Gingerbread Boy. I am hungry and I want to eat you up."

Storyteller: But the Gingerbread Boy ran on saying:

Gingerbread Boy: "Run, run as fast as you can. You can't catch me. I'm the Gingerbread Man."

Storyteller: And run away he did! But the cat ran after the dog who was running after the Little Old Woman who was running after the Gingerbread Boy.
The Gingerbread Boy ran on until he met a pig. The pig said:

Pig: "Stop, stop, Gingerbread Boy. I am hungry and I want to eat you up."

Storyteller: But the Gingerbread Boy ran on saying:

Gingerbread Boy: "Run, run as fast as you can. You can't catch me. I'm the Gingerbread Man."

Storyteller: And run away he did! But the pig ran after the cat who was running after the dog who was running after the Little Old Woman who was running after the Gingerbread Boy.
The Gingerbread Boy ran on until he met a fox by the river. The Fox said:

Fox: "Here, Gingerbread Boy, jump on my back and I will carry you across the river so the pig, the cat, the dog, and the Little Old Woman won't catch you."

Storyteller: The Gingerbread Boy jumped on the Fox's back and the Fox started to swim across the river. The Fox said:

Fox: "The water is getting deeper. Get up on my head, Gingerbread Boy, so you won't get wet."

Storyteller: The Gingerbread Boy got on the Fox's head. Then the Fox said:

Fox: "The water is getting deeper. Get on my nose, Gingerbread Boy, so you won't get wet."

Storyteller: And the Gingerbread Boy got on the Fox's nose. The Fox opened his mouth and in fell the Gingerbread Boy! The fox ate the Gingerbread Boy all up because that's what Gingerbread Boys are for.

STONE SOUP — RETOLD

Storyteller: Once upon a time there was a little old woman who lived in a house by the road. This little old woman was so mean that nobody wanted to live with her, so she lived all alone.

One night there was a knock at her door. When she opened it, there stood a skinny dog. He was so skinny that his ribs stuck out and his poor legs looked like little bird legs. The dog said:

Dog: "Old woman, I am far from home. I have walked for eight days and nights and I haven't had anything to eat. I am so tired and hungry. Please, could I come inside to rest and have something to eat?"

Storyteller: The Old Woman had a big garden with lots of good food in it but she said:

Old Woman: "Go away, Dog. I only have enough food for myself."

Storyteller: And she slammed the door right in the poor Dog's face. The Dog had an idea. He picked up a large stone in his mouth and knocked on the door again. When the Old Woman opened the door, he said:

Dog: "Old Woman, since you have only enough food for yourself, I have brought a stone to make stone soup. Now if you will just wash it off and cook it in a kettle of water we will have a fine stone soup."

Storyteller: The Old Woman said:

Old Woman: "Well, I declare, Dog, I never heard of stone soup."

Storyteller: But the Old Woman did as the Dog asked. She washed the stone and put it in a kettle of water on the stove. Finally, the Dog said:

Dog: "Just give me a big spoon and let me taste our soup."

Storyteller: The Old Woman gave the Dog a spoon and he tasted the soup. He smacked his lips and slurped the soup. He said:

Dog: "My, my! This stone soup is good, but it needs a little something. Do you have a potato?"

Storyteller: The little Old Woman ran out to her garden and got a potato and put it in the kettle.

Dog: "My, my! This stone soup is good, but it still needs a little something. Do you have a carrot?"

Storyteller: The little Old Woman ran out to her garden and got a carrot and put it into the kettle.

The Dog tasted the soup again and he smacked his lips and slurped and slurped.

Dog: "My, my! This stone soup is good, but it still needs a little something. Do you have a tomato?"

Storyteller: The little Old Woman ran out to her garden and got a tomato and put it into the kettle.

The Dog tasted the soup again and said:

Dog: "Now, Old Woman, the stone soup is just right."

Storyteller: The Dog and the Old Woman ate all the stone soup.

Dog: "Thank you, Old Woman, for the good stone soup."

Storyteller: And then the Dog went outside. He laughed so hard about the trick he'd played on the stingy Old Woman that he fell down in the dirt road and rolled over and over.

THE BIG, BIG, TURNIP, SOUTHERN STYLE

Storyteller: Once upon a time there was a Little Old Man. This Little Old Man loved to eat turnips more than anything in the whole world. He ate turnips for breakfast, turnips for lunch, and turnips for supper. He ate turnip soup, turnip salad, and turnip sandwiches, but his favorite thing to eat was (pause) turnip ice cream!

The Little Old Man could never get enough turnip ice cream so he decided to grow his own big, big turnip. He dug a hole, planted a turnip seed and covered it with dirt. The sun shined and the rain rained. Finally, the turnip began to grow.

The Little Old Man decided it was time to pull up the big, big turnip and make himself some turnip ice cream. He pulled and he pulled and he pulled, but it wouldn't come up. So he called the Little Old Woman.

Old Man: "Little Old Woman, come and help me pull up the big, big turnip."

Storyteller: The Little Old Man pulled on the turnip and the Little Old Woman pulled on the Little Old Man. They pulled and they pulled and they pulled, but the turnip wouldn't come up. So the Little Old Man called the girl.

Old Man: "Girl, Girl, come here and help us pull up the big, big turnip. Now y'all pull, hear?"

Storyteller: The Little Old Man pulled on the turnip. The Little Old Woman pulled on the Little Old Man. The girl pulled on the Little Old Woman. (Oh, children: If we help them pull, maybe it will come up. Let's all pull.) They pulled and they pulled and they pulled, but the turnip wouldn't come up. So the Little Old Man called the dog.

Old Man: "Dog, Dog, come here and help us pull up the big, big turnip. Now y'all pull, hear?"

Storyteller: The Little Old Man pulled on the turnip. The Little Old Woman pulled on the Little Old Man. The girl pulled on the Little Old Woman. The dog pulled on the girl. They pulled and the pulled and they pulled, but the turnip wouldn't come up. So the Little Old Man called the cat.

Old Man: "Cat, Cat, come here and help us pull up the big, big turnip. Now y'all pull, hear?"

Storyteller: The Little Old Man pulled on the turnip. The Little Old Woman pulled on the Little Old Man. The girl pulled on the Little Old Woman. The dog pulled on the girl, and the cat pulled on the dog. They pulled and they pulled and they pulled but the turnip wouldn't come up.

They were all just about to sit down and cry because that turnip wouldn't come up, when along came a mouse.

Mouse: "What are y'all doing?"

Old Man: "We're trying to pull up this big, big turnip."

Mouse: "Oh, let me help."

Storyteller: They all laughed at the mouse.

All: "Ha, ha, ha."

Mouse: "Please, please let me help?"

Old Man: "All right, Mouse, you can help. Now y'all pull, hear?"

Storyteller: The Little Old Man pulled on the turnip. The Little Old Woman pulled on the Little Old Man. The girl pulled on the Little Old Woman. The dog pulled on the girl. The cat pulled on the dog. The mouse pulled on the cat. They pulled and they pulled and they pulled. They pulled as hard as they could and the turnip came up!

They took the turnip to the kitchen. They put it into a big pan and cooked it and cooked it. They mashed it all up and poured twenty-one gallons of milk and thirty-six cups of sugar into it. They put it in the freezer.

And what did they make? That's right, they made turnip ice cream. They all ate turnip ice cream until they were about to pop. The little old man patted his tummy and said:

Old Man: "My, my! That sho' was good turnip ice cream."

LITTLE RED RIDING HOOD

Storyteller: Once upon a time there was a little girl named Little Red Riding Hood. She was called that because she always wore a little red cape with a hood on it that her Grandmother had made for her.

One day, Little Red Riding Hood's mother said:

Mother: "Child, your grandmother is sick in bed. I made all these goodies for her so she would feel better. I put them in this little basket for you to take them to her."

Storyteller: She gave the basket of goodies to Little Red Riding Hood and said:

Mother: "Now, Little Red Riding Hood, I want you to go straight to Grandmother's house. Don't stop to play and, whatever you do, don't talk to strangers."

Little Red Riding Hood: "I'll go straight to Grandmother's house and I won't talk to any strangers."

Storyteller: So Little Red Riding Hood started out to Grandmother's house. She had to go through the deep dark woods to get there. She ran through the woods because they were scary.

Finally she came to a green meadow sprinkled with flowers. Little Red Riding Hood forgot she wasn't supposed to stop and play and she started picking the flowers. She was so busy filling her basket with flowers that she didn't see the Big Bad Wolf creep up. The wolf said:

Wolf: "Hello, little girl. What are you doing?"

Storyteller: Little Red Riding Hood said:

Little Red Riding Hood: "I am going to my grandmother's house just over the hill. She is sick in bed and I am taking her some goodies."

Storyteller: The Big Bad Wolf said good-bye to her and ran away over the hill to Grandmother's house. He knocked on the door and said in a little voice:

Wolf: "Grandmother, can I come in?"

Storyteller: Grandmother thought Little Red Riding Hood was at the door and she said:

Grandmother: "Come in, dear. The door is unlocked."

Storyteller: Well! the Big Bad Wolf pushed open the door and ran into Grandmother's house. When she saw it was the Big Bad Wolf, poor Grandmother was scared to death! She got so excited that her night cap and her glasses fell off. She ran out the back door just as the Big Bad Wolf was about to get her, she yelled:

Grandmother: "Help! Help! The Big Bad Wolf is after me."

Storyteller: The wolf said:

Wolf: "She looks too skinny to eat. I'll just wait for Little Red Riding Hood and eat her up."

Storyteller: So the Big Bad Wolf put on Grandmother's night cap and her glasses and got in her bed. He pulled the covers up around his neck and waited for Little Red Riding Hood.

Pretty soon there was a knock at the door. The Big Bad Wolf said in a voice like Grandmother's,

Wolf: "Come in, Little Red Riding Hood, I'm here in my bed."

Storyteller: Little Red Riding Hood skipped right in with the basket of goodies and the flowers for Grandmother.

Little Red Riding Hood: "Grandmother, what big ears you have."

Storyteller: The Big Bad Wolf said:

Wolf: "All the better to hear you with, my dear."

Storyteller: Little Red Riding Hood said:

Little Red Riding Hood: "Grandmother, what big eyes you have."

Wolf: "All the better to see you with, my dear."

Storyteller:Little Red Riding Hood said:

Little Red Riding Hood: "But, Grandmother, what a big mouth you have."

Storyteller: The Big Bad Wolf said:

Wolf: "All the better to EAT you with!"

Storyteller: The wolf jumped out of Grandmother's bed. He chased Little Red Riding Hood all around the house and was just about to catch her, when Grandmother rushed in with a man who had been chopping wood. The man chopped the Big Bad Wolf's head off with his axe and that was the end of him.

TRADITIONAL STORIES

NOAH'S ARK

(Please note: Noah's Ark is a combination of felt and cardboard)

THE ARK FLANNELBOARD

MATERIALS:
—One and one-half yards light blue felt
—One piece of cardboard two by three feet in size
—One-half yard tan felt
—Two (2) by sixteen (16) inch piece of red felt
—One piece each, nine (9) by twelve (12) inch black, white, red, orange, yellow, dark green, dark blue, dark brown felt
—Ruler
—Permanent black marking pen
—Small amount of polyester fiberfill

DIRECTIONS:
1. Cut light blue piece of felt 28" by 40".
2. Place the two- by three-foot piece of cardboard in the center of the light blue felt.
3. Put glue on the edge of the cardboard.
4. Fold the 2" overlap of felt over the edge of the cardboard and press into the glue. You can reinforce the edge by putting masking tape over it.

IMPORTANT: Do not put glue under front of felt because it cuts down on the static electricity that holds the figures on the board.

5. Using the pattern for the ark, cut one top and one bottom from the tan felt and one roof from the red felt.
6. Using the black permanent marker, draw the lumber lines and nail heads as indicated on the pattern.
7. There are names below the lumber lines. These indicate where you will cut slits to insert the story figures.
   a. On the left side, CUT
   —Noah's slot = 2"
   —Noah's Wife's slot = 2½"
   —Kangaroo slot = 2½"

117

—Tiger slot = 4¼”
—Mice slot = 1”
  b. On the right side, CUT
     —Noah's sons' slot = 3¾”
     —Noah's sons' wives' slot = 3½”
     —Elephants' slot = 4¼”
     —Giraffe's slot = 2⅜”

8. After the slots are cut, glue the red roof on top.

9. Cut a piece of dark brown felt 5½ inches by 3 inches to go in the center of the ark.

10. Put glue around the edges of the ark pieces.

11. On the right-hand side of the light blue flannelboard, glue the top, then the brown piece, then the bottom piece, into place.

12. Using the rainbow pattern and instructions in the "Pink Plastic Pig Sisters' Space Adventure," make a felt rainbow without the jelly beans.

13. Cut two white clouds from felt. Glue the polyester fiberfill onto the shapes to give the appearance of clouds.

14. Glue the rainbow onto the left-hand side of the light blue flannelboard.

15. Glue the clouds at the ends of the rainbow.

FIGURES TO USE WITH NOAH'S ARK

MATERIALS:
—One large sheet white tissue paper
—One black fine line permanent marker
—One black medium line permanent marker
—Crayons or oil pastels
—One used foam fabric softener pad or scraps of felt
—Pencil

DIRECTIONS:
1. Using the patterns for Noah's people and animals, take tissue paper and pencil and trace the characters.

2. Place the tissue paper on the DULL side of the poster board.

3. Take the medium line marker and trace over the lines of the characters that you traced in pencil. The permanent marker will "bleed" through the tissue and leave an outline. Take the markers and go over the outlines on the poster board.

4. Color the characters with crayons or pastels.

5. Cut out as you would paper dolls.

6. Glue small pieces of the foam or felt onto back so that cardboard characters will stick to the felt.

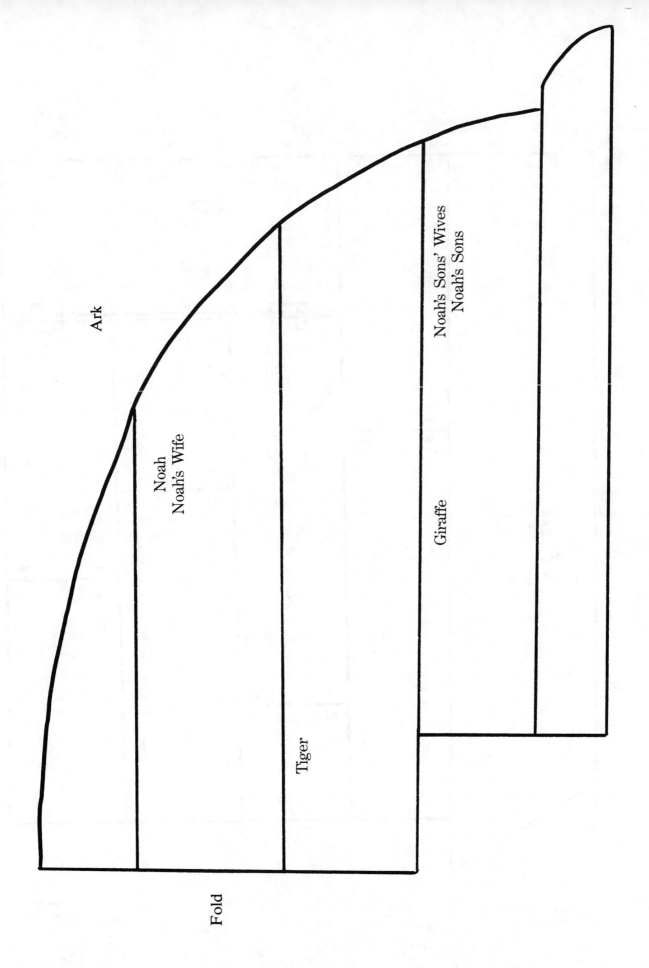

Ark

Noah
Noah's Wife

Tiger

Giraffe

Noah's Sons' Wives
Noah's Sons

Fold

119

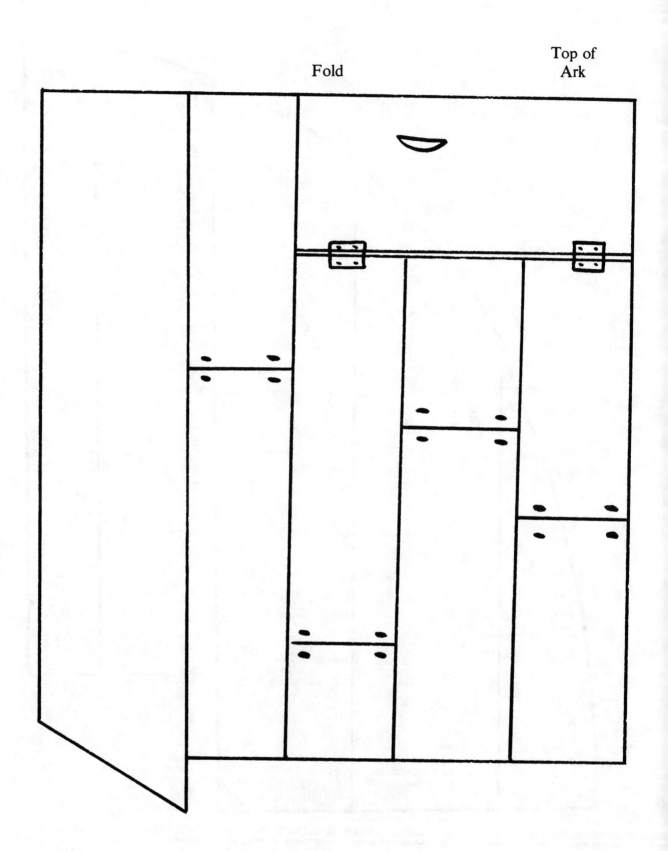

120

Noah's Sons

Noah

Daughters

Mrs. Noah

121

Kangaroo

Dove

Mice

Giraffe

Lions

Elephants

THE THREE BILLY GOATS GRUFF

This story is made on the non-woven interfacing. Instructions can be found in the Winky Witch directions.

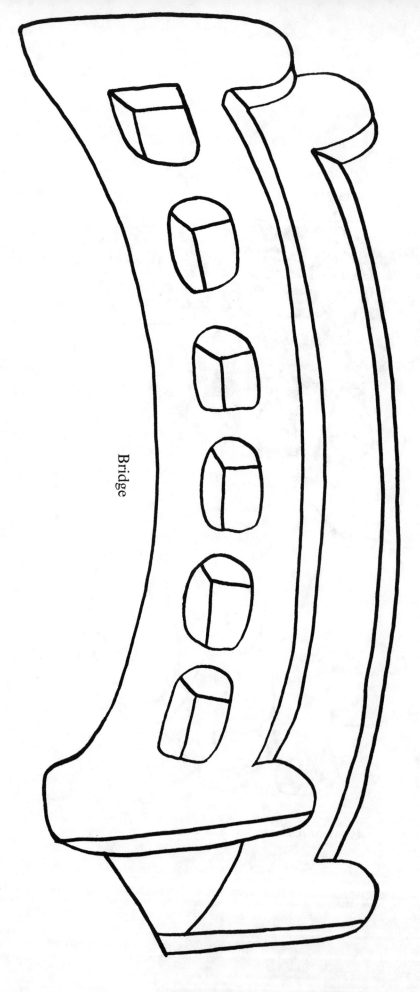

Bridge

Troll

Big Billy Goat

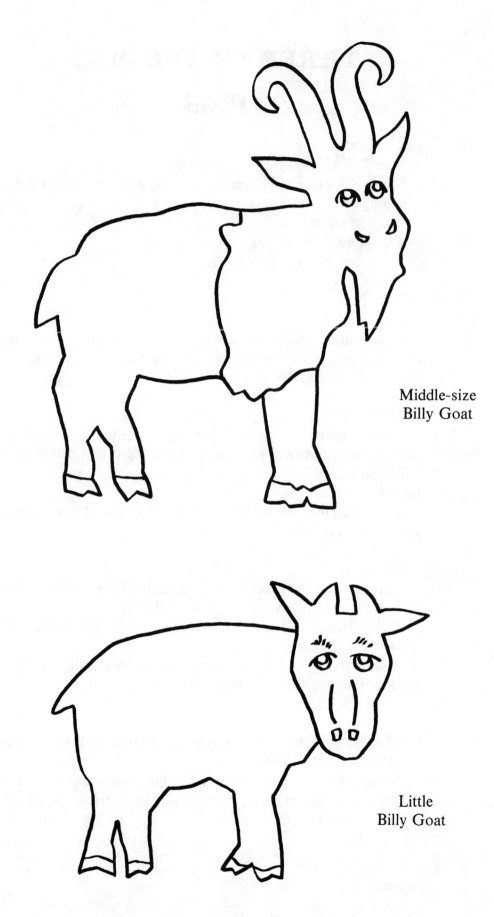

Middle-size
Billy Goat

Little
Billy Goat

127

THREE LITTLE PIGS

PIGS

MATERIALS:
- —Two 9 X 12 inch pieces of pink felt
- —One 3 X 5 inch piece turquoise, yellow, dark brown, tan, bright pink, and light blue felt
- —Scrap of calico
- —Three pair 5mm wiggle eyes
- —Permanent black marking pen

DIRECTIONS:

Basic Pig:

Using pattern, cut three basic pig shapes from pink felt. Cut pig noses from pink felt. Put nose and eyes on pigs' faces, glue into place. Draw nose markings, mouth, and chin with black marking pen.

Pig No. 1:

Using patterns, cut pants from turquoise felt, collar, cuffs, pockets, buttons, and hat from light blue felt, and shirt from calico fabric.

Put on pieces in this order: shirt, pants, collar, cuffs, pockets, and buttons.

Draw markings on hat and buttons. Cut ear slits as indicated on pattern and pull pig's ears through.

Pig No. 2

Using pattern, cut pants and two tie pieces from dark brown felt. Cut shirt, tie knot, buttons, and hat from beige felt.

Put on pieces in this order: shirt, pants, buttons, tie, and tie knot. Draw markings on buttons.

Draw markings on hat with marking pen. Cut ear slits as indicated on pattern. Pull Pig's ears through hat.

Pig No. 3

Using patterns, cut pants, scarf, and buttons from bright pink felt. Cut hat and shirt from yellow felt.

Put on pieces in this order: shirt, scarf, pants, and buttons.

Draw markings on hat. Cut ear slits as indicated on pattern, and pull pig's ears through.

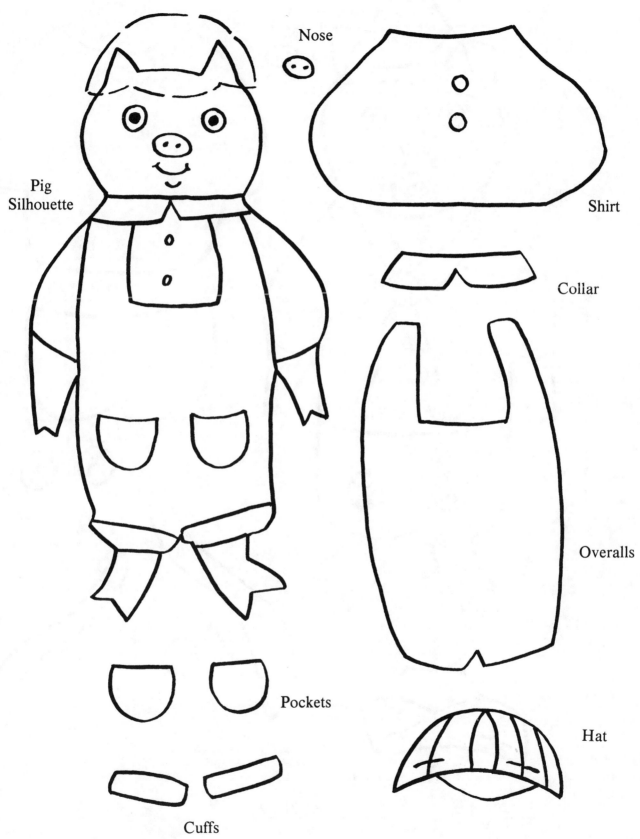

Nose

Pig
Silhouette

Shirt

Collar

Overalls

Pockets

Hat

Cuffs

Pig No. 1

129

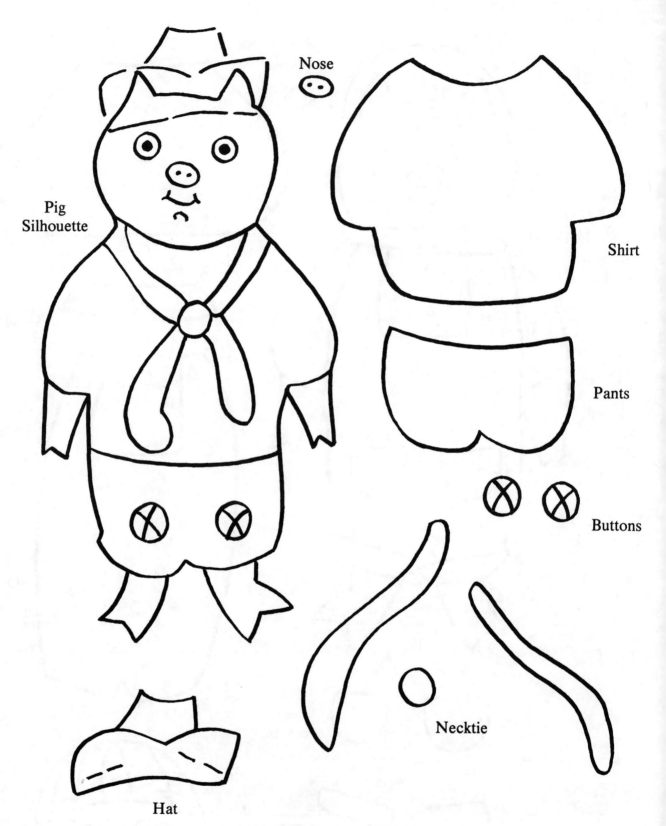

Nose

Pig
Silhouette

Shirt

Pants

Buttons

Necktie

Hat

Pig No. 2

130

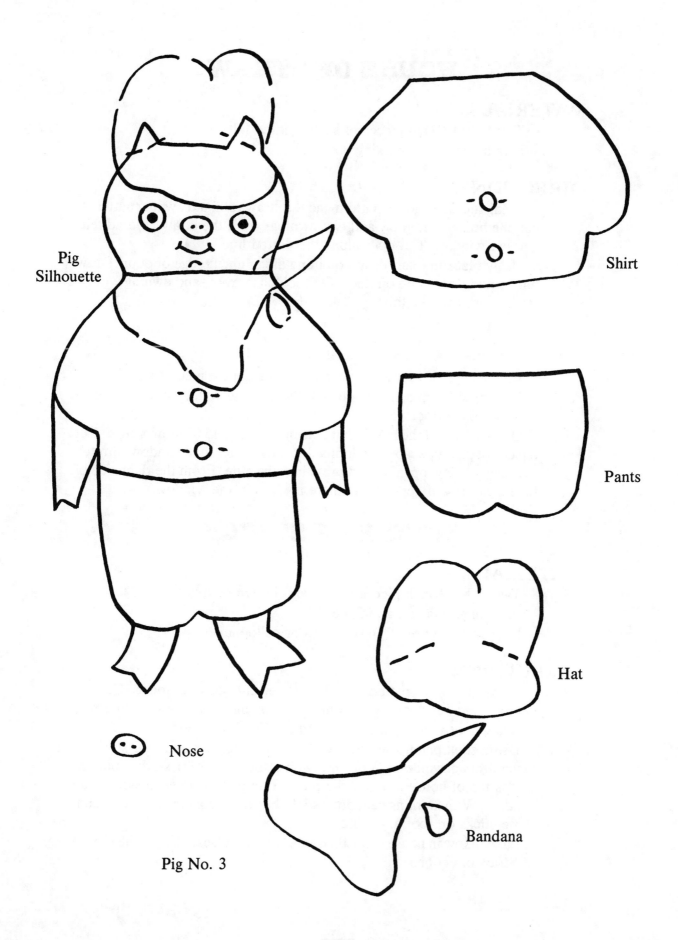

Pig
Silhouette

Shirt

Pants

Hat

Nose

Bandana

Pig No. 3

131

HOUSE OF STRAW

MATERIALS:
—Two 9 X 12 inch pieces of staw-colored felt
—Permanent black marking pen

DIRECTIONS:

Using the basic house pattern and the straw roof and awning patterns, cut one house, one roof, and two awnings from the straw-colored felt. Cut out window. Cut door along the dotted line.

Using black marker, draw solid line along uncut edge of door. Draw hinges and door knob on door. On the house, roof, and awnings, draw straw markings like this:

Fringe edge of roof and awnings to give appearance of straw.

Glue roof to top edge of house. Glue awnings to top edge of window and top of the door.

On back side of the house, put dots of glue around window's edge. Cut a piece of plastic wrap or cellophane ½ inch wider than window. Stretch over the window opening and press into the glue. From the right side of the house, it will appear that there is glass in the window.

HOUSE OF STICKS

MATERIALS:
—Two 9 X 12 inch pieces of medium brown or rust-colored felt
—Permanent black marking pen
—Four-inch square of plastic wrap or cellophane

DIRECTIONS:

Using the basic pattern for the house, cut out one house. Cut out window and cut door along dotted lines as indicated on the pattern.

Draw door markings, hinges, and doorknob on door.

Using stick pattern, cut twelve sticks for the roof and four sticks to place around window. Glue the twelve sticks in a criss-cross pattern across top of house to make the roof. Glue a stick on each side of the window. With marking pen, draw stick shapes on front of house to match those sticks on roof and window.

Put window in house using the same technique described in the House of Straw directions.

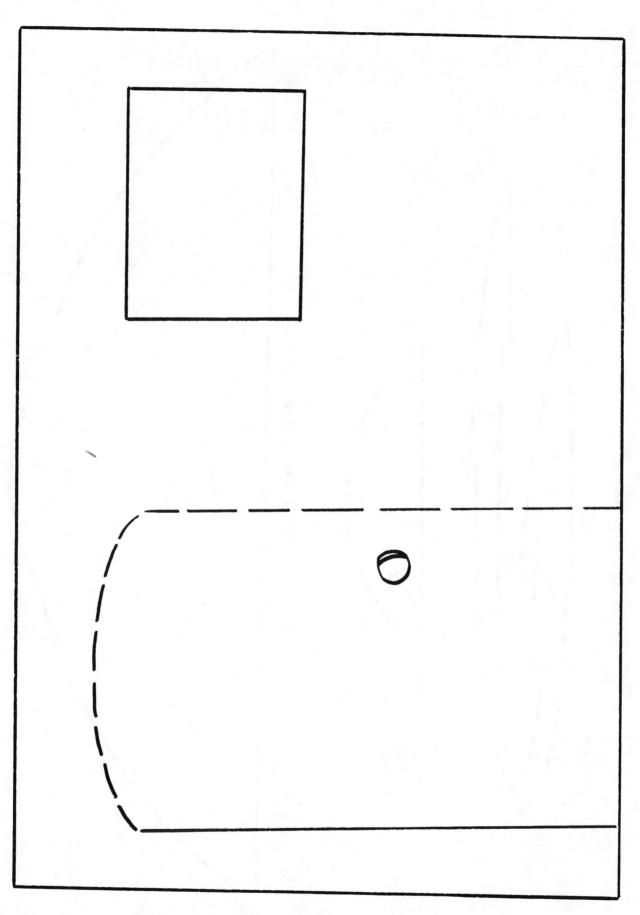

Basic Pig's House Pattern

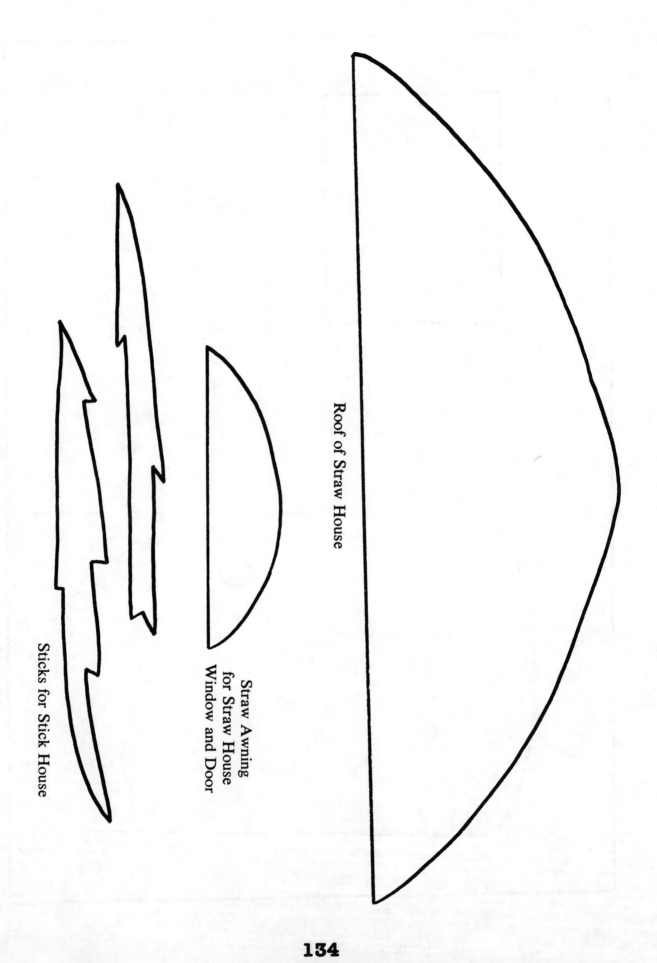

Sticks for Stick House

Straw Awning
for Straw House
Window and Door

Roof of Straw House

HOUSE OF BRICKS

MATERIALS:

—One 9 X 12 inch piece of red felt
—One 9 X 12 inch piece of white felt
—One 2 X 9 inch piece of brown felt
—Scraps of green, blue, purple, yellow, and orange felt
—One 4-inch square of plastic wrap or cellophane

DIRECTIONS:

Using the basic house pattern, cut one house from red felt. Cut out window and cut door along dotted line. With black marking pen, make brick design on house, wood markings on door, door edge, hinges, and doorknob.

Using patterns, cut window box and shutters from white felt. Make an assortment of flowers to fill window box. Glue these pieces in place around window.

Using roof and gable pattern, cut roof pieces from brown felt and gable from white felt. Glue roof to gable, then glue to top edge of brick house.

Put window in house as described in the Straw House directions.

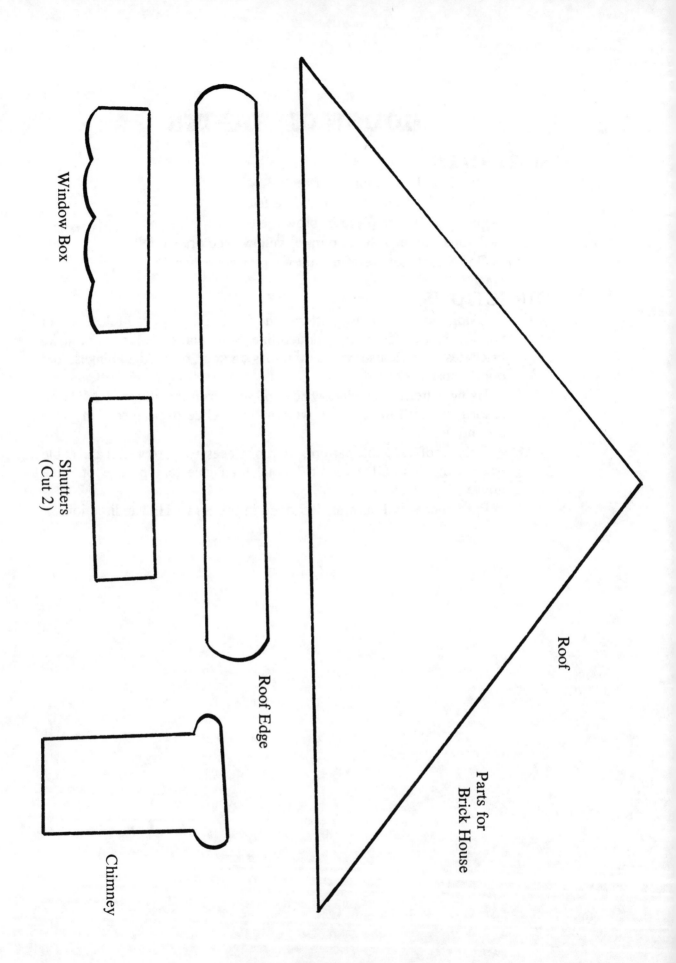

Window Box

Shutters
(Cut 2)

Roof Edge

Chimney

Roof

Parts for
Brick House

136

WOLF

MATERIALS:

—One 4 X 6 inch piece of brown felt
—Scraps of green, red, and white felt
—Three 5mm blue pom-poms
—One 10mm wiggle eye
—Scraps of brown fake fur
—One 5mm black pom-pom

DIRECTIONS:

Using patterns, cut fox silhouette and fox arm from brown felt, vest from green felt, tongue from red felt, and teeth from white felt. Cut tail and eyebrow from brown fake fur.

Put together as follows: vest, arm, blue pom-pom buttons, tail, head, teeth, nose, eye, and eyebrow.

MOTHER PIG

(Use one of the Pink Plastic Pig Sisters for the mother pig.)

Wolf

THE GINGERBREAD BOY

(This story is made on the non-woven interfacing. Instructions for making this kind of figure are found in the Winky Witch story. Use the Old Man and the Old Woman from the Thanksgiving story. Use the dog and cat from the Big, Big Turnip story. Reverse the cat and dog to face right for this story.)

Fox

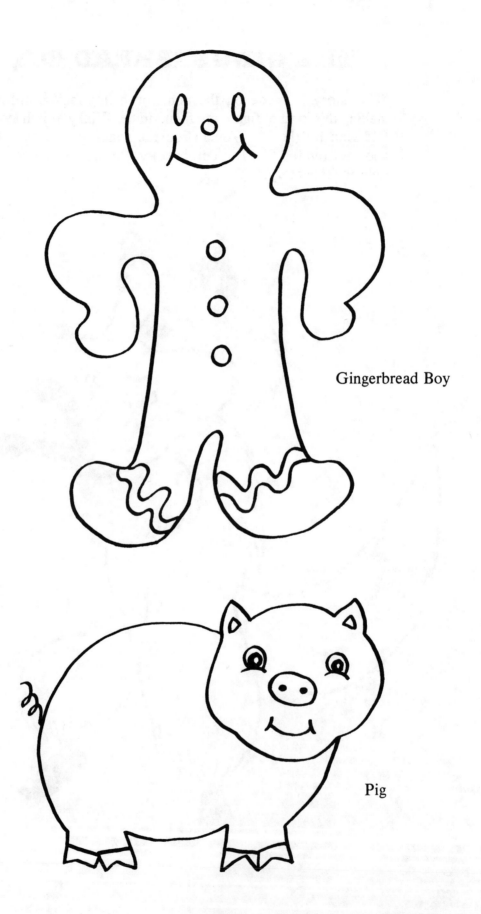

Gingerbread Boy

Pig

STONE SOUP

(Stone Soup is a cardboard story. Instructions for making cardboard figures are included in the "Noah's Ark" story. Use the pattern for the pot in the "Winky Witch" story.)

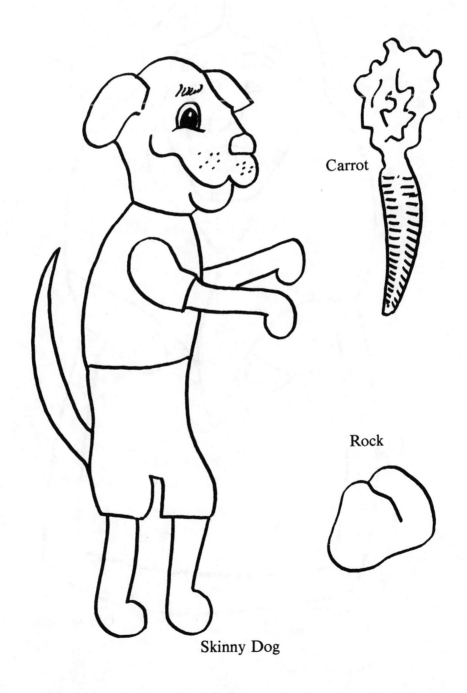

Carrot

Rock

Skinny Dog

Potato

Tomato

Old Woman

BIG, BIG TURNIP (Southern Style)
TURNIP AND HOLE

MATERIALS:
—One 4 X 6 inch piece rust-colored felt
—One 3 X 5 inch piece green felt
—Scraps of white and lavender felt

DIRECTIONS:
Hole: Using pattern, cut hole from rust felt. Make slit for turnip as indicated by dotted lines on pattern. (NOTE: The teacher will put the turnip in the hole before putting it on the flannelboard.

Turnip: Cut one turnip silhouette from green felt, the top of turnip from white felt, and the bottom from lavender felt.

Place white part of turnip on green silhouette, then place lavender on bottom part of turnip, overlapping the white by about ⅛ inch. Glue into place.

OLD MAN

MATERIALS:
—4 X 8 inch skin-colored felt
—Small piece blue calico fabric
—4 X 6 inch piece red felt
—Scraps yellow, gray, and brown felt
—Brown embroidery thread
—One 5 mm wiggle eye
—Permanent black marking pen

DIRECTIONS:
Using pattern, cut man silhouette from skin-colored felt, hat from yellow felt, shoes from brown felt, and beard from gray felt. Cut shirt and knee patch from calico fabric.

Put pieces on the silhouette as follows: shirt, shoes, pants, beard, hat, knee patch, eye, and shoelace.

With black marking pen, put marks on man as indicated on pattern.

Turnip

Hole

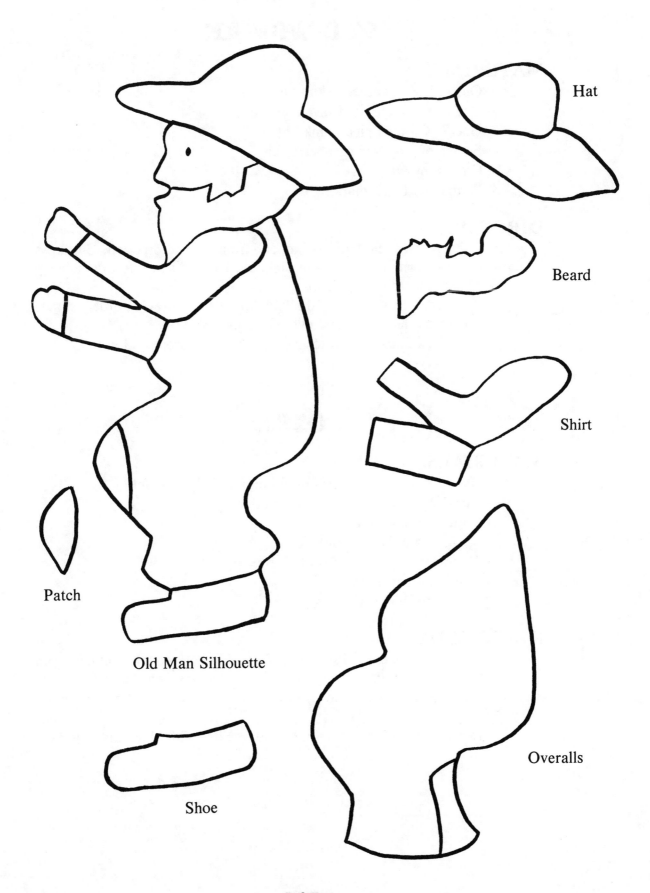

Hat

Beard

Shirt

Patch

Old Man Silhouette

Overalls

Shoe

145

OLD WOMAN

MATERIALS:
—One 4 X 8 inch piece skin-colored felt
—One 3 X 5 inch piece lavender felt
—One 3 X 3 inch piece pink felt
—Scraps of gray and raspberry felt
—One 5 mm wiggle eye
—Permanent black marking pen

DIRECTIONS:
Using pattern, cut lady's silhouette from skin-colored felt. Cut dress from lavender felt, apron from pink felt, hat and shoes from raspberry felt, and hair from gray felt.

Put pieces on skin-colored silhouette in the following order: shoes, dress, apron, hair, hat, and eye. Glue into place.

Use black marking pen to mark eyebrows, apron, and hat.

GIRL

MATERIALS:
—One 6 X 8 inch piece skin-colored and light blue felt
—One 3 X 4 inch piece hair-colored felt
—Scraps of beige felt
—Six inches of ¼-inch ribbon
—Three inches of 1-inch ruffled trim
—One 5 mm wiggle eye
—Permanent black marking pen

DIRECTIONS:
Using pattern, cut girl silhouette from skin-colored felt. Cut hair from hair-colored felt, dress from blue felt, and shoes from beige felt.

Put together in the following order: dress, hair, apron, shoes, hairbow, and eye. Glue into place.

Draw stocking stripes, mouth, and freckles with black marking pen.

Hat

Hair

Apron

Shoe

Old Woman
Silhouette

Hair

Boots

Girl
Silhouette

Dress

148

CAT

MATERIALS:
—One 3 X 5 inch piece white felt
—Scraps of brown and pink felt
—Gray embroidery thread
—Two 5 mm wiggle eyes
—One 5 mm brown pom-pom

DIRECTIONS:
Using pattern, cut one cat silhouette from white felt. Cut head and legs from brown felt.

Place head and legs on cat silhouette. Glue into place.

Make whiskers from 2-inch piece of embroidery thread and place in middle of cat's face. Glue brown pom-pom on top of whiskers for nose. Snip a tiny piece of pink felt for mouth and glue under nose. Glue the two eyes into place.

DOG

MATERIALS:
—One 5 X 9 inch piece brown felt
—One 5 mm pom-pom
—One 5 mm wiggle eye

DIRECTIONS:
Using pattern, cut body silhouette, two legs, and ear from brown felt. Place legs, nose, ear, and eye as shown on pattern and glue into place.

MOUSE

MATERIALS:
—Scraps of gray felt
—One 5 mm black pom-pom
—Two 3 mm wiggle eyes
—One 2-inch piece gray embroidery thread
—One 2-inch piece black embroidery thread

DIRECTIONS:
Using pattern, cut mouse silhouette, head, arm, and leg from gray felt. Take 2" piece of gray embroidery thread and knot one end. Place non-knotted end where tail should be and glue leg over tail. Put arm and head on silhouette and glue into place. Make whiskers from black embroidery thread. Place under black pom-pom nose and glue into place. Glue wiggle eyes in place.

Cat

Head

Legs

Mouse

Ear

Legs

Dog

150

LITTLE RED RIDING HOOD

(Little Red Riding Hood is a non-woven interfacing story. Instructions for making figures from non-woven interfacing are found preceding the Winky Witch story. Make five of each of the trees in the patterns for a total of ten trees. This will make a very "scary" woods for the story.)

Grandma

Woodcutter

151

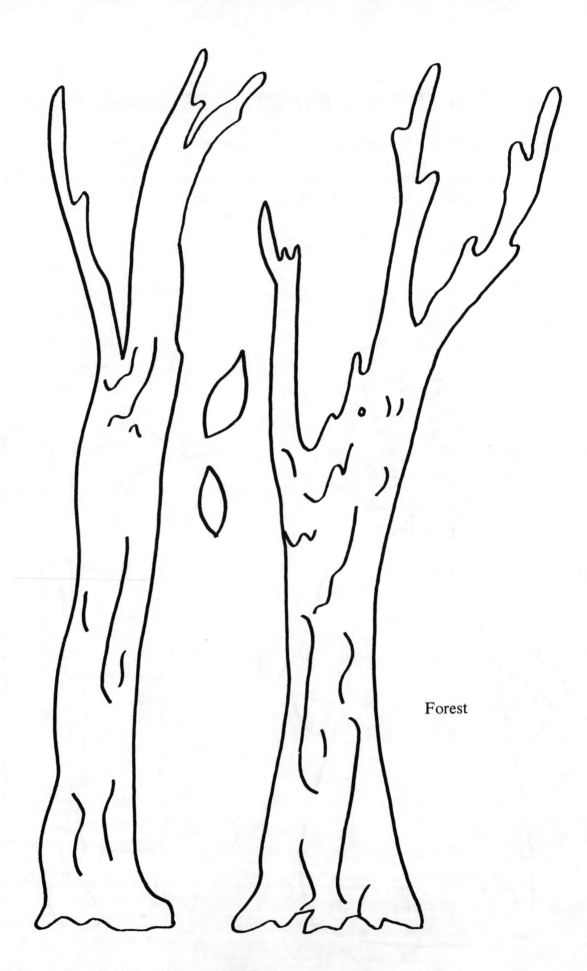

Forest

Mama

Red
Riding
Hood

153

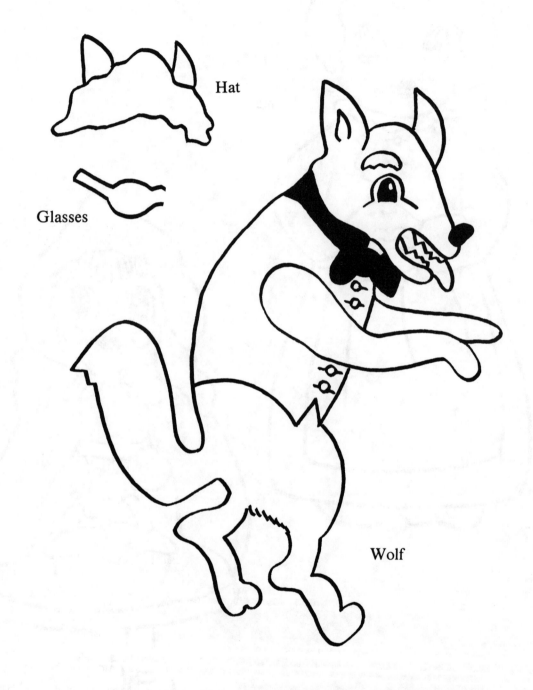

Hat

Glasses

Wolf

154

JUST FOR FUN STORIES

BABY DUCK

Storyteller: One bright sunny morning Mama Duck took the brand new Baby Duck for a walk to see the big world.

Mama Duck walked fast. Baby Duck toddled along behind her. Baby Duck stopped to smell the pretty flowers and Mama Duck went on over a big hill. When Baby Duck looked up, Mama Duck was gone. He called his Mama in his teeny tiny voice.

Baby Duck: "Quack, quack, quack."

Storyteller: But Mama Duck didn't come. So Baby Duck walked on until he met Brother Pig. He said:

Baby Duck: "Please, Brother Pig, will you call my Mama?"

Storyteller: Brother Pig said he'd be glad to call Baby Duck's Mama and he said:

Brother Pig: Oink, oink, oink."

Storyteller: But Mama Duck didn't come. So Baby Duck walked on until he met Brother Rooster.

Baby Duck: "Please, Brother Rooster, will you call my Mama?"

Storyteller: Brother Rooster said he'd be glad to call Baby Duck's Mama and he said:

Brother Rooster: "Cockle-doodle-do."

Storyteller: But Mama Duck didn't come. So Baby Duck walked on until he met Sister Sheep.

Baby Duck: Please, Sister Sheep, will you call my Mama?"

Storyteller: Sister Sheep said she'd be glad to call Baby Duck's Mama and she said:

Sister Sheep: "Baa, baa, baa."

Storyteller: But Mama Duck didn't come. So Baby Duck walked on until he met Sister Cow.

Baby Duck: Please, Sister Cow, will you call my Mama?"

Storyteller: Sister Cow said she'd be glad to call Baby Duck's Mama and she said:

Sister Cow: "Moo, moo, moo."

Storyteller: But Mama Duck didn't come. So Baby Duck walked on until he met great big Duncan Duck.

Baby Duck: Please sir, Duncan Duck, will you call my Mama?"

Storyteller: Great big Duncan Duck said he'd be glad to call Baby Duck's Mama, and he said in his great big duck voice:

Duncan Duck: "Quack, quack, quack!"

Storyteller: And this time Mama Duck came running back over the hill to the little Baby Duck.

THE PREPOSTEROUS PINK PEOPLE EATER

Storyteller: Sam David had been playing hard all morning. He was hot and tired so he sat down to rest under the big shade tree. His eyes were feeling sleepy. All at once he heard a tiny, squeaky voice calling from beind a bush.

Preposterous Pink People Eater: "Wake up! Wake up, little boy! I'm hungry."

Storyteller: Sam David looked around and there stood a tiny man. He was pink all over. He had a fat little belly and he was trying very hard to look mean. Sam David laughed when he saw him. This made the tiny pink man very mad.

Preposterous Pink People Eater: "Little boy, don't you laugh at me. I am ugly and I am mean. I am the Preposterous Pink People Eater and I am going to eat you for my lunch."

Storyteller: Sam David said:

Sam David: "Please don't eat me for lunch. Why don't we go in my mama's kitchen and cook you something good for lunch? I know, let's make a Pink Pie."

Storyteller: The Preposterous Pink People Eater rubbed his fat little belly and said:

Preposterous Pink People Eater: "Yum, yum. Pink Pie sounds good for lunch."

Storyteller: Sam David and the Preposterous Pink People Eater went into Sam David's mama's kitchen. They got out a big bowl and began to put good things in it. They put in six gallons of milk, ten cups of sugar, twenty-two eggs and eleven gallons of strawberry ice cream.

The Preposterous Pink People Eater jumped up on the side of the bowl and began to stir as hard as he could. Pink Pie filled up the big bowl. Then it ran over the bowl onto the table. Then it ran off the table onto the floor. Then it ran out of the kitchen into the living room. Then it ran out of the living room into the yard. Then it ran into Sam David's sandbox. It filled up the whole sandbox. Sam David cried:

Sam David: "Stop, stop, stop stirring the Pink Pie."

Storyteller: The Preposterous Pink People Eater stopped stirring and said:

Preposterous Pink People Eater: "What's the matter? What are you yelling about?"

Storyteller: Sam David said:

Sam David: "Look what a mess you've made! Pink Pie is all over the kitchen, the living room and the yard and it's even in my sandbox. My mama will be very mad when she sees this mess. She might even spank us both. Oh, what am I going to do?"

Storyteller: The Preposterous Pink People Eater said:

Preposterous Pink People Eater: "Don't worry, little boy. I will eat up all of this pink pie."

Storyteller: He pulled out a very long straw and put it in the sandbox. He began to suck.

Preposterous Pink People Eater: "Slurp, slurp, slurp."

Storyteller: He sucked all the pink pie out of the sandbox, slurp, then he sucked all the Pink Pie out of the living room, slurp. Then he sucked all the Pink Pie out of the kitchen, slurp. Then he sucked all the Pink Pie out of the bowl.

Preposterous Pink People Eater: "Slurp, slurp, slurp."

Storyteller: Then his fat little belly was a fat BIG belly.

Preposterous Pink People Eater: "Yum, yum. I'm not going to be a Preposterous Pink People Eater anymore. You can call me the Preposterous Pink Pie Eater. Good-bye, little boy."

Storyteller: Sam David blinked his eyes and the little man was gone.

SILAS SNAKE

Storyteller: This is Silas Snake. He is a nice gentle snake. He never bites anyone. He doesn't even have any teeth. He has a lovely long red tongue, though, and when he sticks it out he says, S S S S. But poor Silas Snake is a very sad snake. He doesn't have any friends at all and he gets very lonely.

One morning Silas Snake slid out of bed very early. He said:

Silas Snake: "I am tired of being lonely. Today I am going to find a friend."

Storyteller: Silas slid along through the grass to Mr. Owl's house. Mr. Owl is very wise and Silas Snake asked:

Silas Snake: "Please, Mr. Owl, will you tell me how to find a friend? I am such a sad and lonely snake and I want to find a friend today."

Storyteller: Mr. Owl thought and thought and then he said:

Mr. Owl: "Silas Snake, you do not have a friend because you look so mean. People are afraid of snakes. You must do something to make yourself look friendly."

Storyteller: Before Silas could ask what he could do to look friendly, Mr. Owl closed his eyes and went to sleep. Silas Snake slid on his way. He finally came to a town. He said:

Silas Snake: "Maybe I'll find a way to make myself look friendly in this big town."

Storyteller: Just then he saw a lady coming out of a hat store. She was wearing a beautiful red hat and she certainly looked friendly. Silas slid right up to the lady. He stuck out his long red tongue and smiled and said:

Silas Snake: "S S S S."

Storyteller: The poor lady was scared to death. She screamed:

Lady: "Help! Help! A snake is after me!"

Storyteller: She ran away in such a hurry that her hat fell off. Silas said:

Sila Snake: "That pretty red hat made the lady look friendly. I think I'll just put it on and see if it will make me look friendly."

Storyteller: And that's just what he did. He looked at himself in a store window.

Silas Snake: "I declare, I look friendly in this red hat. Now I'll find a friend."

Storyteller: He saw a little boy waiting to cross the street and he slid right up to him. He stuck out his long red tongue and smiled and said:

Silas Snake: "S S S See my pretty red hat."

Storyteller: That little boy took one look at Silas Snake and ran away crying.

Boy: "Mama, Mama! Help! Help! A snake is after me."

Storyteller: Silas Snake said:

Silas Snake: "I guess that little boy doesn't like red hats. I'll just go in this hat store and buy me a blue hat."

Storyteller: And that's just what Silas did. He put the blue hat on top of the red hat. He looked at himself in a store window and said:

Silas Snake: "I declare I look friendly in my red and blue hats. Now I'll find a friend."

Storyteller: He saw a fat man sitting in the sun eating peanuts, and he slid right up to him. He stuck out his long red tongue and smiled.

Silas Snake: "S S See my pretty hats."

Storyteller: That man took one look at Silas Snake, threw his peanuts up in the air and ran away yelling:

Man: "Help!"

Storyteller: Silas Snake said:

Silas Snake: "Well, I never! I guess that man doesn't like red and blue hats. I'll try one more time. I'll buy me a yellow hat."

Storyteller: And that's just what Silas did. He put the yellow hat on top of the blue hat on top of the red hat. He smiled at himself in the store window and said:

Silas Snake: "I do declare! I look mighty friendly now in my red and blue and yellow hats. Now I'll find a friend."

Storyteller: Just then he saw a little girl walking along pushing her doll buggy and he slid right up to her. He stuck out his long red tongue and smiled and said:

Silas Snake: "S S See my pretty hats."

Storyteller: That little girl took one look at Silas, snatched up her doll and ran away yelling:

Girl: "Help! Help! A snake is after me!"

Storyteller: Silas Snake said:

Silas Snake: "Well, I never! I guess the people in this town don't like snakes wearing hats."

Storyteller: Silas Snake curled up in a ball and began to cry. He had tried so hard to look friendly, but nobody wanted to be his friend. Poor Silas. Just then he heard a noise, " S S S S." When Silas looked up there was a beautiful green girl snake. She stuck out her long red tongue and said:

Serita Snake: "My name is Serita Snake. Your hats are beautiful and you are a friendly looking snake. Would you like to be my friend?"

Storyteller: Silas Snake had finally found a friend! Serita Snake would be his friend. He was so happy that he gave her his yellow hat and they slid away together. Silas Snake will never be lonely again.

BABY DUCK

DUCKS

MATERIALS:
—One 9 X 12 inch piece white felt
—Scraps of yellow and orange felt
—Three 5 mm wiggle eyes

DIRECTIONS:
Using duck patterns, cut duck silhouettes and wings from white felt. Cut beaks from yellow felt. Cut feet from orange felt.

Put pieces into place as indicated on pattern, then glue into place.

MR. SHEEP

MATERIALS:
—One 9 X 12 inch piece cream colored felt
—Scraps of black felt
—One 5 mm wiggle eye

DIRECTIONS:
Using pattern, cut sheep silhouette from cream felt. Cut legs, ears, and muzzle from black felt.

Place pieces and eyes on sheep as indicated on pattern. Glue in place.

MR. ROOSTER

MATERIALS:
—One 3 X 4 inch piece of gold felt
—Scraps of red, yellow, orange, and green felt
—One 5 mm wiggle eye

DIRECTIONS:
Using pattern, cut Mr. Rooster silhouette from gold felt, wing from green felt, comb and wattle from red felt, beak from yellow felt, and feet from orange felt. Place all pieces on silhouette as indicated on pattern, then glue into place.

MRS. COW

Use the cow pattern in the Christmas story to make the cow for this story.

Wing

Daddy
Duck

Beak

Feet

Wing

Wing

Beak

Baby
Duck

Beak

Mama
Duck

162

Muzzle

Ears

Legs

Mr. Sheep

163

Comb

Beak

Mr. Rooster

Wattle

Feet

Wing

164

THE PREPOSTEROUS
PINK PEOPLE EATER

MATERIALS:
—One 4 X 6 inch piece pink felt
—Scraps of three other shades of pink
—One ½-inch pink pom-pom
—Scrap of pink calico fabric
—One pair 10mm pink wiggle eyes
—Small amount of polyester fiberfill

DIRECTIONS:
Using pattern, cut body silhouette, head, and hands from pink felt. Cut pants, shoes, and mouth from different shades of pink felt. Cut shirt (arms) from pink calico. Make two small bows from embroidery thread.

Place the pieces on in this order: Pants, hands, shirt, head, eyes, nose, mouth, shoes, and shoe bows.

Glue the pieces onto the base. Take the fiberfill and place around pink wiggle eyes and pom-pom nose. Preposterous should appear bald-headed with a moustache. Glue fiberfill in place.

PINK PIE

MATERIALS:
—Small piece of tan and pink felt
—Black permanent marker

DIRECTIONS:
Using pattern, cut pie-pan silhouette out of the pink felt. Cut pie crust from the tan felt. "Snip" out the three small holes in crust with fingernail scissors so pink will show through. Draw markings on pie crust with black marking pen. Glue tan piece on top of pink piece.

Preposterous

Shoes

Arms

Mouth

Face

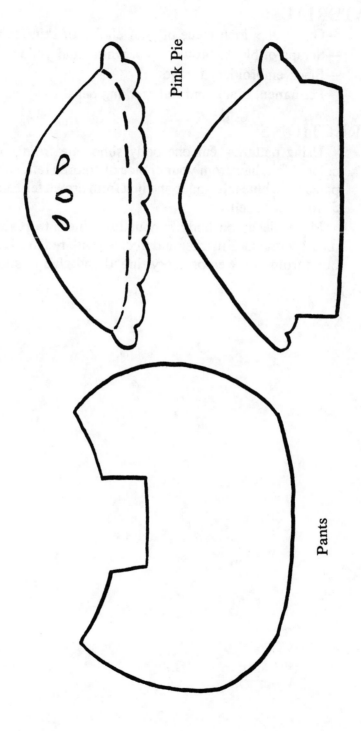

Pink Pie

Pants

SAM DAVID

MATERIALS:

—One 3 X 9 inch piece of your choice of skin-colored felt
—Scraps of black, brown, blue, white, and yellow felt
—Black embroidery thread
—Permanent black and red marking pens

DIRECTIONS:

Using patterns, cut one body silhouette from your choice of skin-colored felt, hair from your choice of colored felt, shirt from yellow felt, pants from blue felt, shoes and belt from brown felt, and eyes and number 5 from black felt.

Place pieces on body silhouette. Glue into place. Draw nose and mouth with black marker and freckles with red marker. Make shoestring bows from black embroidery thread and glue to shoes.

TABLE

MATERIALS:
—One piece 4 X 8 inch tan felt

DIRECTIONS:
Using pattern, cut table from tan felt.

BOWL

MATERIALS:
—One 2 X 3 inch piece blue felt
—One 2 X 3 inch piece pink felt

DIRECTIONS:
Using pattern, cut whole bowl silhouette from pink felt. Cut bowl from blue felt.
Glue blue bowl over pink silhouette.

SANDBOX

MATERIALS:
—One 4 X 8 inch piece dark brown felt
—One 4 X 8 inch piece tan felt

DIRECTIONS:
Using pattern, cut silhouette of box with sand in it from tan felt. Cut box from brown felt and glue on top of tan felt.

TREE

(Use the pattern for the tree in the bear stories.)

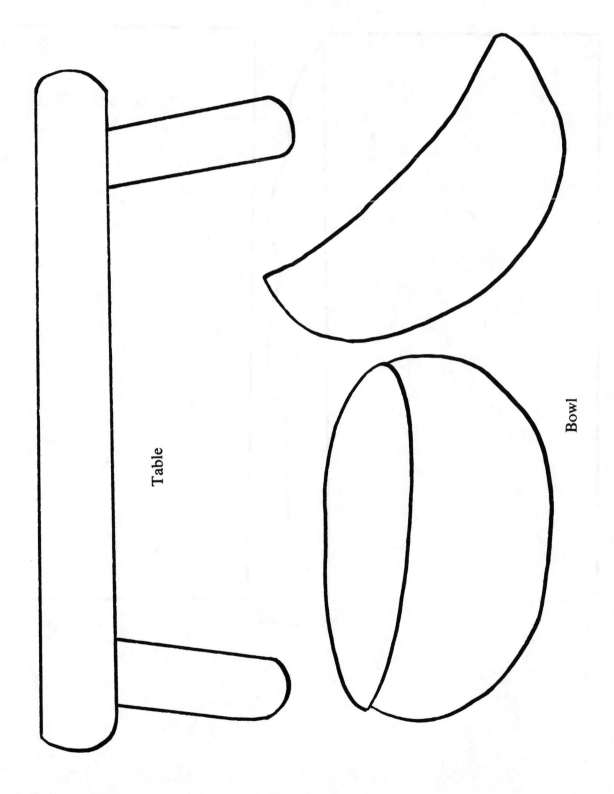

Table

Bowl

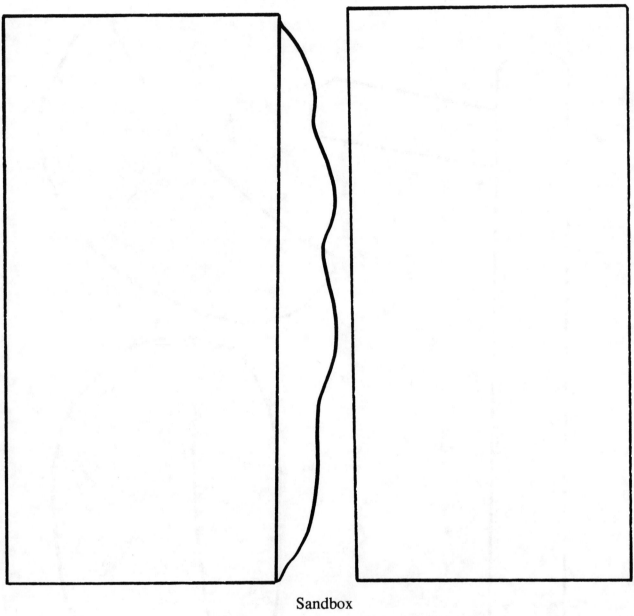

Sandbox

SILAS SNAKE

Silas Snake is a story made on the non-woven interfacing. Use the directions in "Winky Witch" to make this story. Use the pattern for Aunt Em in the Thanksgiving story for the lady in this story. Use the pattern for Sam David in "The Preposterous Pink People Eater" for the little boy.

Owl

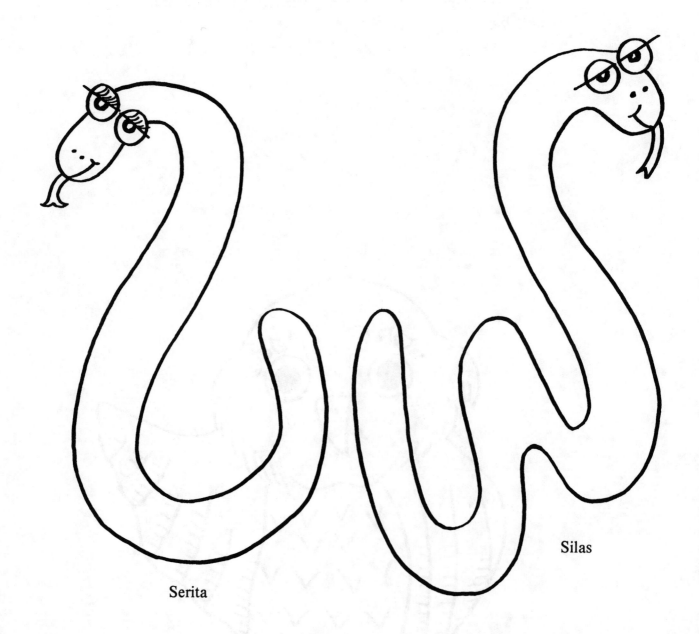

Serita

Silas

Hats

Fat
Man

175

Little
Girl

HOLIDAY STORIES

WINKY WITCH

Storyteller: Long, long ago and far, far away deep in the dark woods there was a scary cave. This was the cave where the witches lived.

The old mean witches had long crooked noses with a big wart on the end. They had great big yellow teeth that made them look ugly when they laughed their scary laugh. They wore long black witch dresses and tall black witch hats.

Now, there was a tiny witch named Winky Witch who lived in the scary cave with the big mean witches. Winky Witch wore a long black witch dress, too, but it was too long and she always tripped on it. Her tall black witch hat was too big and it always fell down over her eyes. And, Winky Witch was not ugly. She couldn't scare anybody. She wasn't a good witch at all. She was even scared of the dark.

One dark, dark Halloween night the witches came out of their scary cave. They called their black cats and got out their big black pot. The witches put frog tails and fleas and spider webs into the pot. Then they danced around it, stirring it with a big spoon. They laughed their scary laugh.

Witches: (In a scary voice) "Ha, ha, ha, ha! Double bubble, double bubble. Tonight we'll make trouble. Ha, ha, ha, ha!"

Storyteller: Winky Witch danced around the pot with the big witches. She tried to laugh a scary laugh, too, but it sounded like this:

Winky Witch: (in a tiny voice) "Ha, ha, ha, ha! Double bubble, double bubble, Tonight we'll make trouble. Ha, ha, ha, ha!"

Storyteller: Then the witches called their black cats and jumped on their broomsticks and flew high up in the dark sky. Winky Witch flew on her little broomstick right behind the big witches. Soon the witches saw a bright light down on the ground below. They flew down close to the light.

It was a candle in a Jack O'Lantern. Then the witches played a trick! They blew out the Jack O'Lantern's candle just like this:

Witches: (Pretend to blow out the candle)

Storyteller: Then the witches laughed their scary laugh.

Witches: "Ha, ha, ha, ha! Double bubble, double bubble. Tonight we'll make trouble. Ha, ha, ha, ha."

Storyteller: The witches flew back up high in the dark sky to look for more Jack O'Lanterns. It got darker and darker and the big witches flew faster and faster. They flew too fast for little Winky Witch. Soon she was all alone in the dark sky. Winky Witch was scared. Just then she saw a bright light far down on the ground. She said:

Winky Witch: "I'll fly down there where it's not dark."

Storyteller: When she got near the light, Winky Witch saw it was a Jack

178

O'Lantern. She stood up as tall as she could and tried to look mean like the big witches so she could scare the Jack O'Lantern.

Winky Witch: (in a tiny voice) "Ha, ha, ha, ha! Double bubble, double bubble. Tonight I'll make trouble. I'm going to blow out your candle."

Storyteller: Just as she was about to blow out the Jack O'Lantern's candle, her tall black witch hat fell down over her eyes and she tripped over her long black witch dress and she fell right down. The Jack O'Lantern wasn't scared a bit. He laughed and said:

Jack O'Lantern: (in a deep voice) "Ho, ho, ho, little witch. If you play a trick on me and blow out my candle it will be dark."

Storyteller: Winky Witch was scared of the dark and she didn't really want to blow out the nice Jack O'Lantern's candle.

Winky Witch: "I am a witch and witches are supposed to play tricks on Halloween. What can I do if I don't blow out your candle?"

Storyteller: The Jack O'Lantern said:

Jack O'Lantern: "You can go trick or treating with me and the children will give us candy. I will light up the dark for you with my candle!"

Storyteller: And that's just what they did. When you go trick or treating on Halloween night, if you look really hard, you just may see Winky Witch and the Jack O'Lantern.

BOBBY JOE'S THANKSGIVING DINNER

Storyteller: Once upon a time I knew a family. These are the people in the family. This is Grandma and Grandpa. Here are Mama, Daddy, and Aunt Em. These are the children. The big brother's name is C.W. The girls are Billie Sue and Peachy. The little brother is Bobby Joe. One night Grandma said:

Grandma: "Thanksgiving will be here before we know it. It's about time we started planning our Thanksgiving dinner. I'll bake the turkey and make the dressing. What will you do for Thanksgiving, Aunt Em?"

Aunt Em: "Well, I make mighty good rolls and cranberry sauce. Billie Sue, what about you?"

Billie Sue: "I could make some apple pies."

Storyteller: And Daddy said,

Daddy: "I had a mighty good crop of apples this year. I'll bring the apples for the apple pies."

Storyteller: And Mama said:

Mama: "I'll fix the vegetables. Let's see, we could have green peas, squash and sweet potatoes with marshmallows on the top. Grandpa, what will you do for Thanksgiving?"

Grandpa: "I'll bring in some wood and build a big fire in the fireplace. C. W., what about you?"

C.W.: "Well, we have a whole lot of pecans on the pecan tree. I'll fill up a big basket with pecans."

Storyteller: Peachy said:

Peachy: "Well, I'm too little to cook, but I could set the table."

Storyteller: Little Bobby Joe had listened to everybody tell what they'd do for the Thanksgiving dinner, but he couldn't think of a thing to do. Then he had an idea. He said:

Bobby Joe: "What I can do is help everybody!"

Storyteller: Grandma said,

Grandma: "You'll be the best helper in the family, Bobby Joe."

Storyteller: So the family started getting ready for their Thanksgiving dinner. Grandma put the turkey in the oven and started on the dressing. Little Bobby Joe stood on a chair and helped Grandma crumble the cornbread for the dressing.

Then Daddy and Bobby Joe went down to the cellar to get the apples. Bobby Joe helped Daddy carry the apples upstairs.

Billie Sue made the apple pies and Bobby Joe sprinkled cinnamon and sugar on the apples.

Aunt Em rolled out the dough for the rolls and Bobby Joe helped her cut them out and put them on the pans to rise.

Mama cooked the green peas and the squash and the sweet potatoes. Bobby Joe put marshmallows on top of the sweet potatoes.

Grandpa brought in the logs to make the fire in the fireplace. Bobby Joe brought in the kindling and crumpled up the paper to help the fire get started. C.W. took the big basket out in the yard to the pecan tree. Bobby Joe helped him fill it with pecans.

Peachy put the lace tablecloth on the table and then put out a plate for each person. While she put the forks and knives by the plates, Bobby Joe put a spoon by each plate.

The house smelled good with Thanksgiving cooking. Finally Grandma said:

Grandma: "The dinner is ready. Come sit down."

Storyteller: The family was hungry by now and they all sat down at the big table covered with the dinner they had all helped to make. They bowed their heads and they all held hands. Together they said,

Family: "We are thankful for our family and our good Thanksgiving dinner."

Storyteller: Then they ate the big Thanksgiving dinner they had all helped to make. Grandma was right. Little Bobby Joe was the very best helper in the family.

JESSICA THE CAT'S CHRISTMAS TALE

Storyteller: This is Jessica, my cat. Jessica has lived in our house as long as I can remember. Jessica and I have shared many quiet times together and she has told me many wondrous things.

Jessica told me this story that she had heard from her greatest of grandmother cat who was named Jesse.

Jesse lived long, long ago in a town called Nazareth. She belonged to a young girl named Mary. Mary was a gentle, kind girl who always gave Jesse milk from the family goat that she milked. Mary would brush Jesse's long, brown fur and make her feel very loved.

Mary grew up and married a man named Joseph. Joseph was a carpenter who built furniture and cabinets. He knew Mary loved Jesse and so he built a special box for Jesse to sleep in.

As time went by, Joseph and Mary had to take a trip to the town of Bethlehem to pay their taxes. Mary was going to have a baby and she was very sad about leaving her family. Joseph thought that she might not be so lonely if Jesse went with them to Bethlehem.

Joseph saddled the donkey and tied Jesse's special box onto the saddle. They traveled a long way and were very tired when they got to Bethlehem. Joseph went to many hotels, but all the rooms were filled. One kind man told Joseph that he and Mary could sleep in his barn that he had just put fresh, clean hay in.

Joseph helped Mary off the donkey and took Jesse's box down and they went into the barn. They spread their blankets on the fresh, clean hay so that they could sleep. They were very tired.

During the night Jesse awoke to the most wondrous sight. A bright star was shining over the barn and in the manger there was a new baby sleeping. Jesse asked the cow:

Jesse: "What has happened?"

Storyteller: The cow answered with a soft:

Cow: "Moooooo"

Storyteller: Jesse asked the donkey:

Jesse: "What has happened?"

Storyteller: The donkey replied in a most regal way:

Donkey: "Hee, Haw!"

Storyteller: Jesse asked the sheep:

Jesse: "What has happened?"

Storyteller: The sheep gave a soft:

Sheep: "Baa, baa."

Storyteller: Jesse asked the doves in the top of the barn:

Jesse: "What has happened?"

Storyteller: The doves fluttered their wings and sang:

Doves: "Coo-coo, Coo-coo."

Storyteller: Jesse heard beautiful singing and went to sit beside Mary. Mary looked down and smiled and said:

Mary: "Jesse, we now have a little boy named Jesus to look after and care for."

Storyteller: Jesse rubbed against Mary's leg and purred (make a purring sound). Now Jesse knew what had happened. A beautiful new baby had been born this night. When the shepherds came to the barn with their sheep and the wise kings came riding their camels Jesse smiled her best cat smile for she knew that on this special night the world had been truly blest.

MRS. EASTER CHICKEN

Storyteller: Do you know where the Easter Bunny gets Easter eggs? Well, of course, bunnies don't lay eggs. Chickens do. There is a special chicken who lays Easter eggs for the Easter bunny. Her name is Mrs. Easter Chicken. Mrs. Easter Chicken lives on a farm in a chicken house with all the other chickens. The other chickens sit on their nests and lay plain white eggs, the kind you eat for breakfast. But Mrs. Easter Chicken has a magic nest. When she sits on her magic nest, she lays Easter eggs . . . red and yellow and pink and blue Easter eggs.

Now, Mrs. Easter Chicken has a real problem. She loves to eat. One year right before Easter, Mrs. Easter Chicken ate too many goodies. She ate candy bars, angel food cake, chocolate ice cream, strawberry shortcake, lemon pie, banana pudding, blueberry muffins, waffles with maple syrup, a hot fudge sundae, a vanilla milkshake and pancakes with ice cream and butterscotch sauce! But the worst was yet to come!

The day before Easter, she got on her magic nest to lay Easter eggs, just like she always did. She laid beautiful Easter eggs . . . red and yellow and pink and blue eggs. Lots of Easter eggs. But!! When Mrs. Easter Chicken tried to get off her magic nest, she was stuck. She was so fat from all the goodies she'd eaten that she couldn't get off her magic nest. Mrs. Easter Chicken said:

Mrs. Easter Chicken: "Well, I do declare, I seem to be stuck to my magic nest."

Storyteller: The other chickens shook their heads, flapped their aprons and clucked:

Other Chickens: "My, my. Poor Mrs. Easter Chicken."

Storyteller: Early Easter morning Mr. Easter Bunny came hippity-hopping to the chicken house to fill up his basket with Easter eggs.

Easter Bunny: "Get up please, Mrs. Easter Chicken. I need my Easter eggs."

Storyteller: Mrs. Easter Chicken said,

Mrs. Easter Chicken: "I do declare, Mr. Easter Bunny, I seem to be stuck to my magic nest. I can't get up."

Storyteller: The other chickens shook their heads, flapped their aprons and said:

Other Chickens: "My, my. Poor Mrs. Easter Chicken."

Storyteller: The Easter Bunny said:

Easter Bunny: "Oh, dear! What will I do?"

Storyteller: The dog heard all the commotion and came to see what was going on. The Easter Bunny said:

Easter Bunny: "I beg your pardon, Mr. Dog, but we need some help. Mrs. Easter Chicken is stuck to her magic nest. How can I get her up?"

Mr. Dog: "Put your arms around her and pull hard."

Storyteller: The Easter Bunny put his arms around her and pulled as hard as he could, but still Mrs. Easter Chicken was stuck to her magic nest. The chickens shook their heads, flapped their aprons and clucked:

Other Chickens: "My, My. Poor Mrs. Easter Chicken."

Storyteller: The cat heard all the commotion and came to see what was going on. The Easter Bunny said:

Easter Bunny: "I beg your pardon, Mr. Cat, but we need some help. Mrs. Easter Chicken is stuck to her magic nest. How can I get her up?"

Mr. Cat: "Put your arms around her and shake her."

Storyteller: The Easter Bunny put his arms around Mrs. Easter Chicken and shook her as hard as he could, but Mrs. Easter Chicken was still stuck to her magic nest. The other chickens shook their heads, flapped their aprons and said:

Other Chickens: "My, my. Poor Mrs. Easter Chicken."

Storyteller: The pig heard all the commotion and came to see what was going on. The Easter Bunny said:

Easter Bunny: "I beg your pardon, Mr. Pig, but we need some help. Mrs. Easter Chicken is stuck to her magic nest. How can I get her up?"

Mr. Pig: "Turn the magic nest upside down and she will fall out."

Storyteller: The Easter Bunny turned the magic nest upide down, but Mrs. Easter Chicken was still stuck to her magic nest. The other chickens shook their heads, flapped their aprons and clucked:

Other Chickens: "My, my. Poor Mrs. Easter Chicken."

Storyteller: Well, all the commotion in the chicken house had stirred up the dust. Mrs. Easter Chicken's nose began to tickle. It tickled and tickled. All at once Mrs. Easter Chicken sneezed.

Mrs. Easter Chicken: "Kerr-chooo!"

Storyteller: Up she came! The other chickens flapped their aprons and said:

Other Chickens: "Thank goodness Mrs. Easter Chicken came unstuck!"

Storyteller: The Easter Bunny filled his basket with the red and yellow and pink and blue Easter eggs. He said:

Easter Bunny: "Thank you very much, Mrs. Easter Chicken."

Storyteller: He hippity-hopped away to hide the Easter eggs for the children. Mrs. Easter Chicken said:

Mrs. Easter Chicken: "Well, I do declare! I guess I'll have to go on a diet."

WINKY WITCH

MATERIALS:

—One yard heavy weight non-woven interfacing like pelon. The one with a smooth surface is easiest to use.
—One permanent black fine line marker
—One permanent black medium line marker
—One box of crayons; the more colors, the more variety one can have in coloring the characters.

DIRECTIONS:

Using the patterns for Winky Witch, place the non-woven interfacing over them and trace with the medium line marker. Use the fine line for detail and features.

Color the figures with the crayons.

Heat an iron to the highest setting. Place the figures between two sheets of newspaper and press with the iron to set the colors in the fabric.

Cut the figures from the non-woven interfacing. They are now ready to use on the flannelboard.

(Note: Use the cat pattern in "Mrs. Easter Chicken")

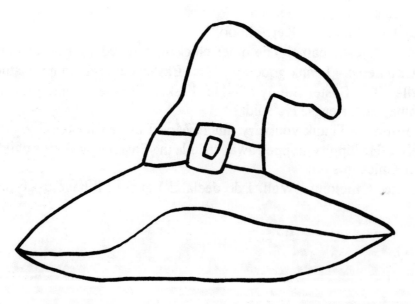

Hat

Broom

Winky

187

Old Witch
(Make Several)

188

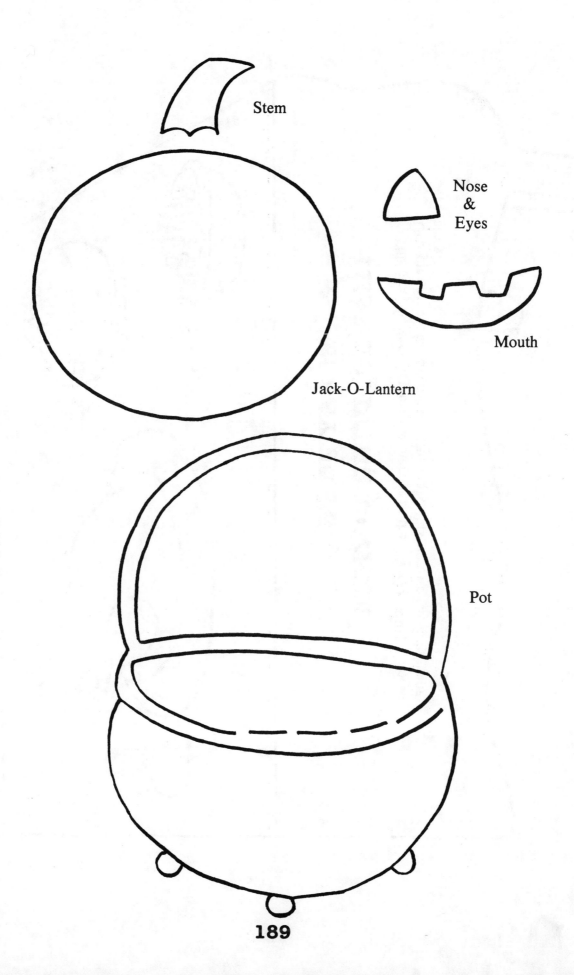

Stem

Nose
&
Eyes

Mouth

Jack-O-Lantern

Pot

189

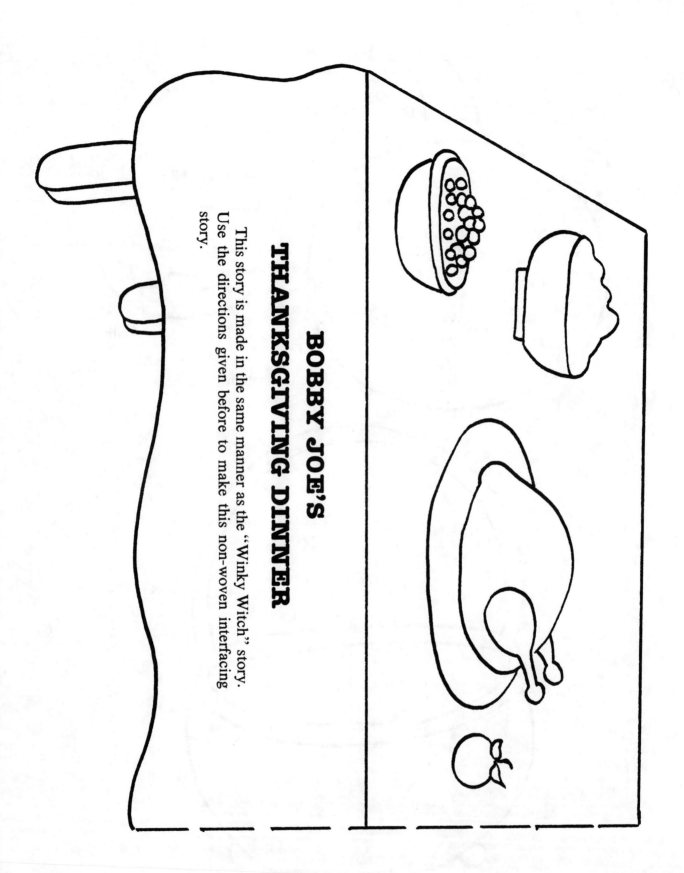

BOBBY JOE'S
THANKSGIVING DINNER

This story is made in the same manner as the "Winky Witch" story. Use the directions given before to make this non-woven interfacing story.

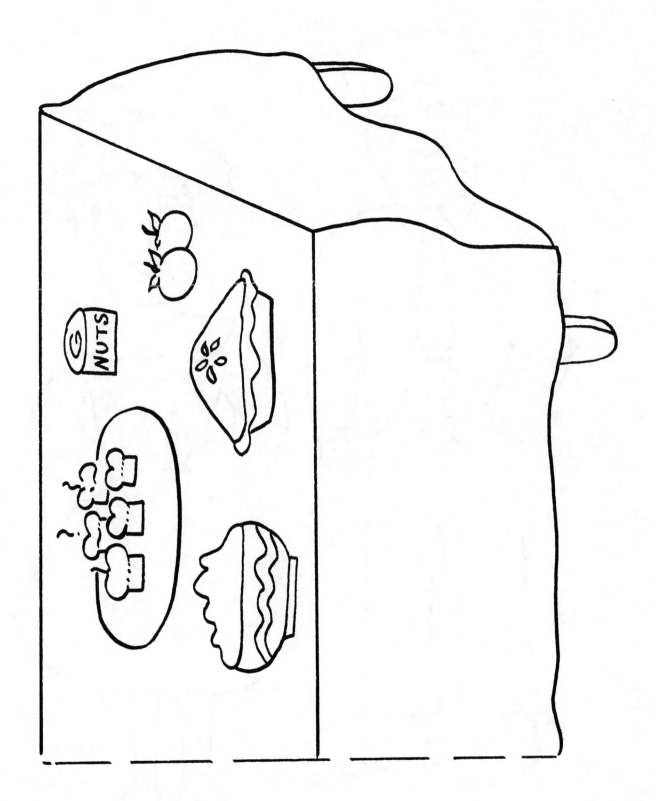

Daddy

Mama

Grandpa

Grandma

Aunt Em

Billie Sue

Bobby Joe

C.W.   Peachy

196

JESSICA THE CAT'S CHRISTMAS TALE

MARY

MATERIALS:
- —One 4 X 6 inch piece dark blue felt
- —One 4 X 6 inch piece white felt
- —Scraps of pink, white, black, red, and light blue felt
- —Fine line permanent black marking pen

DIRECTIONS:

Using pattern, cut body silhouette from dark blue felt. This will serve as the base onto which all parts will be glued. Cut dress sleeves from light blue felt, shawl from white felt, face and hands from pink felt.

Place all pieces on body silhouette. When pieces are aligned to your satisfaction, glue them to base.

Draw eyes, nose, and hand markings with fine line pen. Cut a small "snip" of red felt and glue in place for mouth.

JOSEPH

MATERIALS:
- —One piece 9 X 12 inch dark green felt
- —Scraps of beige and pink felt
- —Fine line permanent black market

DIRECTIONS:

Using pattern pieces, cut one body silhouette from dark green felt. Cut sleeves from dark green felt, face and hands from pink felt, hair, beard, and moustache from beige felt.

Place all pieces on base, then glue into place as indicated on pattern.

Draw facial features with black marking pen.

Mary's completed silhouette

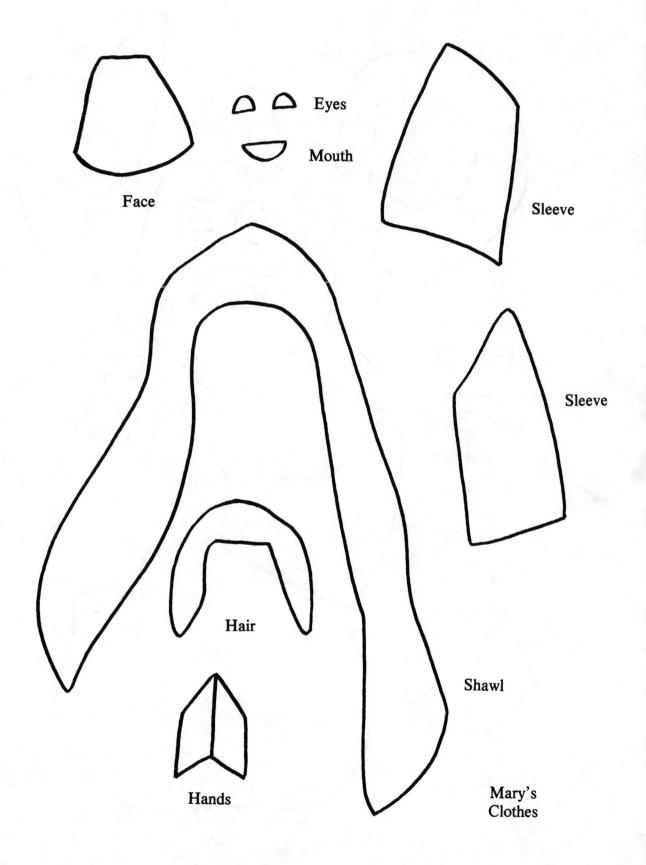

Eyes

Mouth

Face

Sleeve

Sleeve

Hair

Shawl

Hands

Mary's
Clothes

199

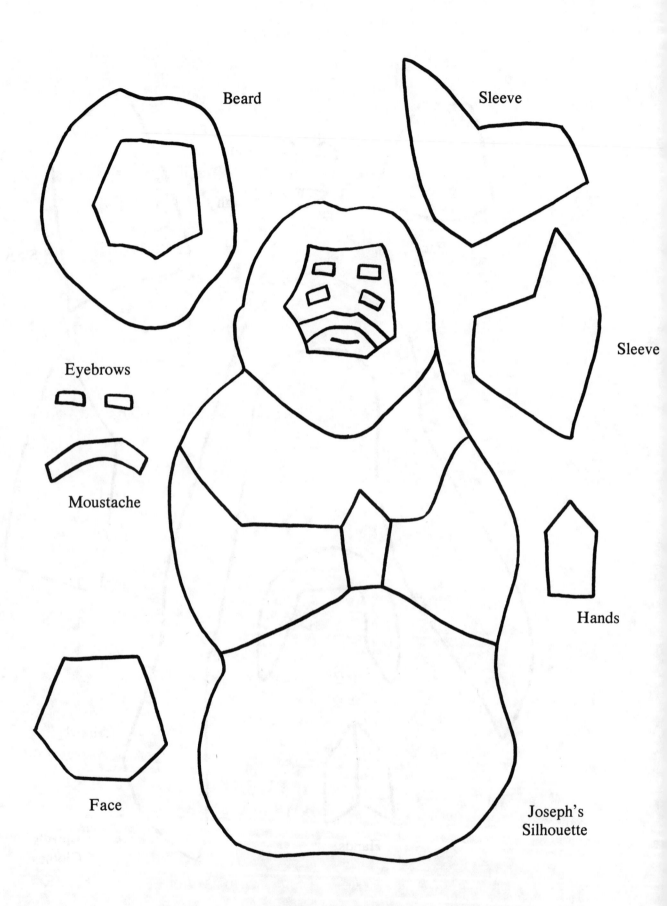

Beard

Sleeve

Sleeve

Eyebrows

Moustache

Hands

Face

Joseph's
Silhouette

200

MANGER

MATERIALS:

—One 4 X 6 inch piece gold and tan felt

DIRECTIONS:

Using patterns, cut manger from tan felt and hay from gold felt.

Fringe edges of gold felt. (To fringe, snip into felt with scissors approximately ½ inch every ⅛ inch.)

Glue hay onto manger.

STABLE

MATERIALS:

—One 9 X 12 inch piece dark brown felt
—Black permanent marking pen

DIRECTIONS:

Using pattern, cut two side pieces, two roof pieces, and two beam pieces.

Put wood markings on the stable pieces.

Place them on the flannelboard as indicated in the following diagram.

PALM TREE

MATERIALS:

—One 9 X 12 inch piece tan and dark green felt
—Black permanent marking pen

DIRECTIONS:

Using pattern, cut tree trunk from tan felt and three palm branches from green felt.

Draw markings on tree tunk and palm branches as indicated on the pattern.

Glue the three palm branches to the top of the tree trunk. The branches should hang down.

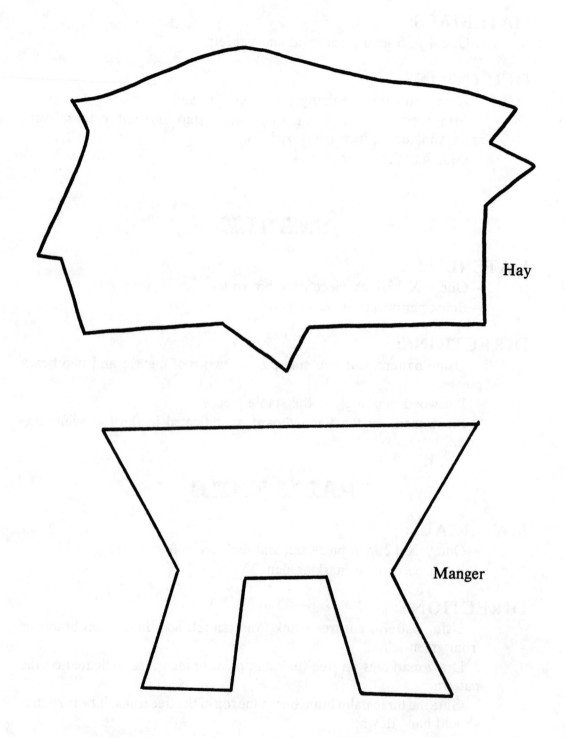

Hay

Manger

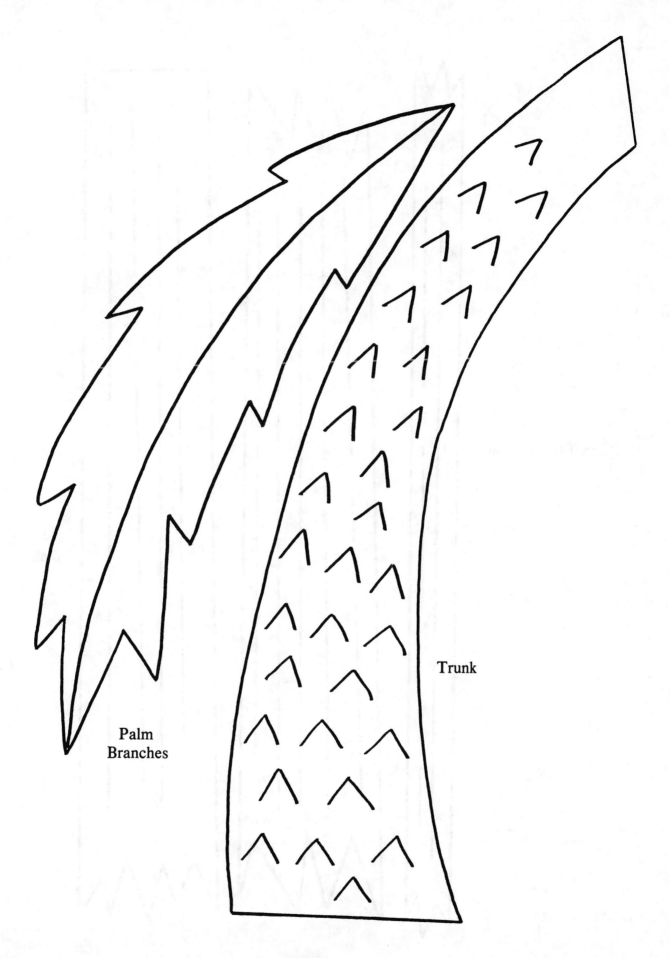

Palm
Branches

Trunk

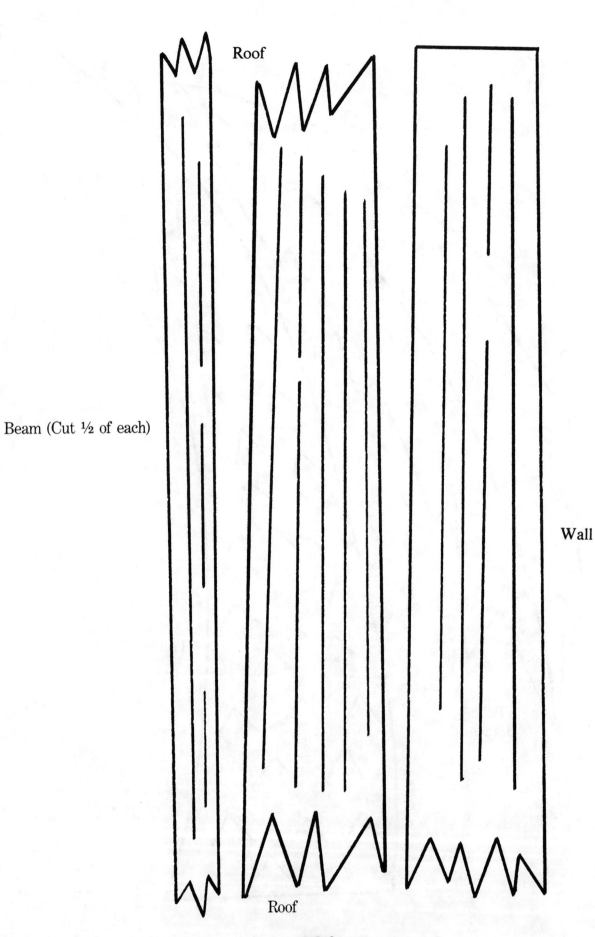

Roof

Beam (Cut ½ of each)

Wall

Cut two
of
each

Roof

BABY JESUS

MATERIALS:

—One 2 X 4 inch piece of light blue felt
—Scraps of pink felt
—Two small brown beads
—Fine line permanent black marking pen

DIRECTIONS:

Using pattern pieces, cut Baby Jesus body shape from light blue felt. Cut face from pink felt.

Glue face to body shape. Glue brown beads as indicated for eyes. Draw mouth with black marking pen.

(NOTE: Use the CAT pattern without the tie in "Mrs. Easter Chicken." Use the SHEEP pattern in "Baby Duck.")

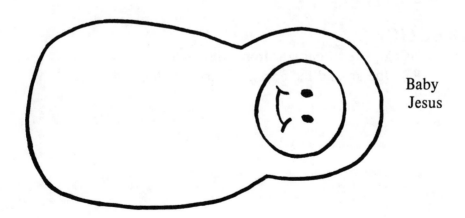

Baby
Jesus

DOVE

MATERIALS:
- —Scraps of white felt
- —Small black beads

DIRECTIONS:

Using the pattern, cut three doves and their wings from white felt. Glue the wings and black bead for eye as indicated on the pattern.

JESSICA'S BOX

MATERIALS:
- —Scrap of tan felt
- —Black permanent marking pen

DIRECTIONS:

Cut one box shape from tan felt and draw wood markings with black marker as shown on the pattern.

STAR

MATERIALS:
- —One 4 X 6 inch piece of white felt
- —Silver glitter

DIRECTIONS:

Using pattern, cut star from white felt.
Put glue around the edge and cover with silver glitter.

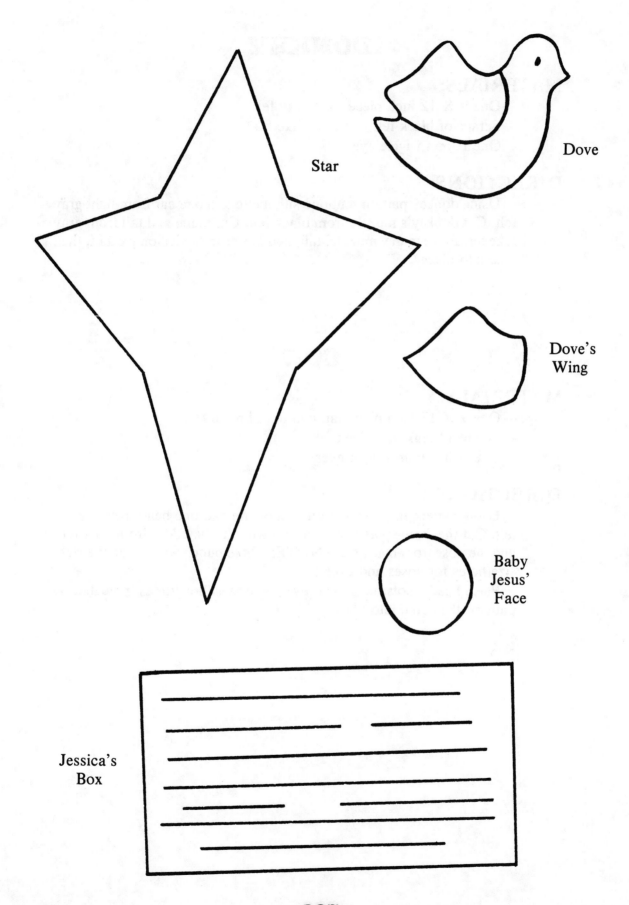

Star

Dove

Dove's
Wing

Baby
Jesus'
Face

Jessica's
Box

DONKEY

MATERIALS:
—One 9 X 12 inch piece light gray felt
—Scraps of black felt and gray fake fur
—One 10mm wiggle eye

DIRECTIONS:
Using donkey pattern, cut one silhouette and one ear from light gray felt. Cut donkey's muzzle from black felt. Cut mane and tail from gray fake fur. Place mane, muzzle, tail, and eye as indicated on pattern, then glue into place.

COW

MATERIALS:
—One 9 X 12 inch piece tan and dark brown felt
—Scraps of pink and black felt
—One pair 10mm wiggle eyes

DIRECTIONS:
Using pattern for cow, cut one silhouette and one head from the tan felt. Cut the three spots from dark brown felt, the udder from pink felt, and the nose from black felt. (NOTE: a hole punch will punch the right size holes for noses and eyes.)

Place head, spots, nose, and eyes on cow silhouette as indicated on pattern, then glue into place.

Mane

Ear

Muzzle

Mane

Tail

209

Cow Silhouette

Cow's
Head

MRS. EASTER CHICKEN

MRS. EASTER CHICKEN AND HENS

MATERIALS:
—One 9 X 12 inch piece white felt
—Scraps of red and orange felt
—Four 5mm wiggle eyes
—Four 1-inch pieces of 1-inch ruffled trim

DIRECTIONS:
Using patterns, cut one Mrs. Easter Chicken silhouette and three hen silhouettes from white felt.

Cut the combs from red felt and beaks from orange felt.

Place combs, beaks, wings, aprons (the 1-inch pieces of ruffled trim) and eyes where indicated on the pattern, then glue into place.

NESTS

MATERIALS:
—One 3 X 4 inch piece dark green felt
—One-half yard dark green 1-inch ruffled eyelet trim
—One 6 X 8 inch piece tan and yellow felt
—Green glitter

DIRECTIONS:
Using nest silhouette, cut one green and three tan.

To make the magic nest, use the green nest and glue two rows of the green eyelet trim at the bottom of the nest. Put glue on the edges of the eyelet and sprinkle green glitter onto it.

To make the hens' nests, cut three straw coverings from yellow felt. Fringe edges as described in the making of the manger in the Christmas story. Glue straw to tan nests.

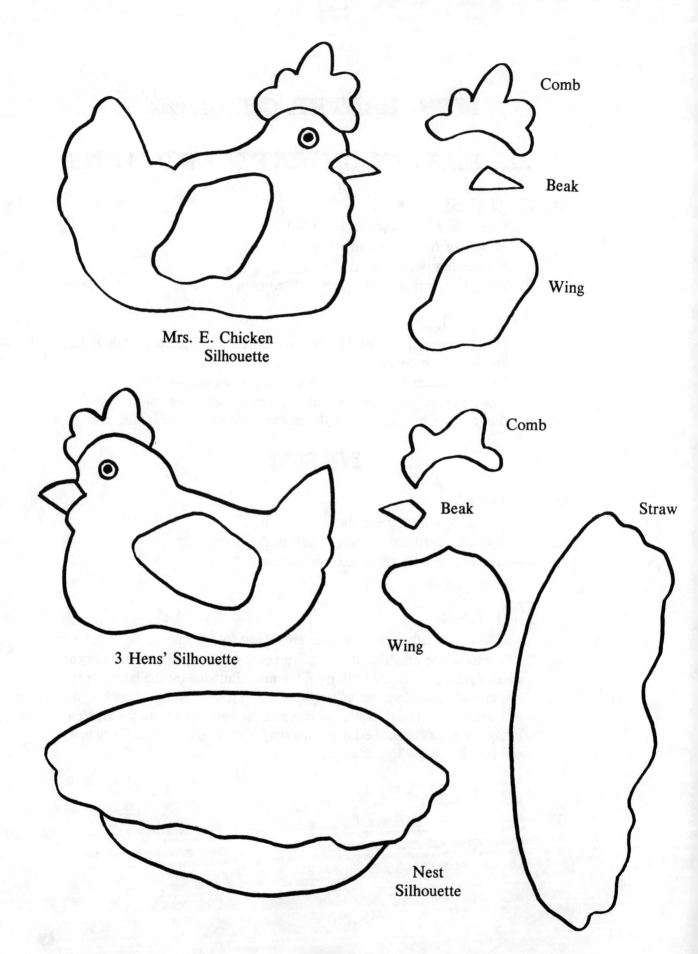

Comb

Beak

Wing

Mrs. E. Chicken
Silhouette

Comb

Beak

Straw

Wing

3 Hens' Silhouette

Nest
Silhouette

EASTER BUNNY AND BASKET

MATERIALS:

—One 9 X 12 inch piece gray felt
—Scraps of brown, tan, red, yellow, pink, white, green, blue, red, orange, and yellow felt
—One ½-inch white pom-pom
—Black embroidery thread
—Two 10 mm oval wiggle eyes

ALTERNATE VERSION:

—One 9 X 12 inch piece gray felt
—Scraps of brown, tan, red, yellow, pink, white, green, blue, and orange felt
—One ½-inch white pom-pom
—Black embroidery thread
—Two 10 mm oval wiggle eyes

DIRECTIONS:

Using pattern, cut rabbit silhouette and arm from gray felt, two ear inserts from pink felt, brown nose, two white felt teeth, and one red felt tie to make the rabbit.

Using patterns, cut basket shape from tan felt, grass from yellow felt, and eggs from assorted colors of felt.

To make rabbit, place all felt pieces and eyes on silhouette. Cut a 2-inch piece of embroidery thread and use three of the pieces to make whiskers. Place these under nose. Glue all pieces and eyes into place. Glue pom-pom for tail.

To make basket, place grass and eggs as indicated on pattern. Glue into place.

Arm

Ear

Nose

Teeth

Bow Tie

Grass

Eggs

Basket

214

MRS. PIG

MATERIALS:
—One 9 X 12 inch piece pink felt
—Scraps of gold, green, and purple felt
—One pair 10mm blue wiggle eyes
—Black permanent marking pen

DIRECTIONS:
Using pattern, cut one pig silhouette, head, and nose from pink felt. Place pieces as indicated on pattern. Glue into place.

Draw nose markings and smile with black marker.

Cut hat from yellow felt. Cut flower from purple and green felt. Cut ear slots with fingernail scissors. Glue flower to hat.

When glue on pig has dried, pull ears through slots on the hat as indicated on the pattern.

MR. CAT

MATERIALS:
—One 5 X 9 inch piece gold felt
—Scrap of calico fabric
—One pair 5mm wiggle eyes
—Scrap of brown felt
—Black embroidery thread

DIRECTIONS:
Using pattern, cut cat silhouette, leg, and head from gold felt. Cut necktie from calico fabric. Punch one circle from brown felt for nose.

Place all pieces and eyes on cat body. Make whiskers as described for the Easter Bunny in "Mrs. Easter Chicken." Glue all pieces into place.

MR. DOG

MATERIALS:
—One 9 X 12 inch piece tan felt
—Scraps of red and black felt
—Scrap of calico
—One 8mm wiggle eye

DIRECTIONS:
Using pattern, cut dog's silhouette, head, ear, and leg from tan felt. Punch nose from black felt. Cut tongue from red felt. Make bandana for dog's neck from calico fabric.

Put all pieces in place as indicated on the pattern. Glue pieces in this order: bandana, head, ear, whiskers, nose, eye, tongue, and leg.

Hat

Pig
Silhouette

Pig Nose

Pig Head

Cat
Silhouette

Head

Leg

Necktie

Nose

Tongue

Dog's Head

Dog's Leg

Bandana

218

BIBLIOGRAPHY

Allstrum, E., 1957. *Let's Play a Story.* New York: Friendship Press.

Ames, L.B., and F.L. Ilg, 1976. *Your Four Year Old.* New York: Delacorte Press.

Ames, L.B., and F.L. Ilg, 1976. *Your Three Year Old.* New York: Delacorte Press.

Anderson, P.S., 1963. *Storytelling with the Flannelboard, Book One.* Minneapolis: T.S. Dennison and Co.

Anderson, P.S., 1970. *Storytelling with the Flannelboard, Book Two.* Minneapolis: T.S. Dennison and Co.

Bauer, C.F., 1977. *Handbook for Storytellers.* Chicago: American Library Association.

Bettelheim, B., 1976. *The Uses of Enchantment, The Meaning and Importance of Fairy Tales.* New York: Alfred A. Knopf.

Brainerd, C.J., 1978. *Piaget's Theory of Intelligence.* Englewood Cliffs: Prentice Hall, Inc.

Chandler, C.A., R.S. Lourie, and A.D. Peters, 1968. *Early Child Care.* New York: Atherton Press.

Cundiff, R.E., and B. Webb, 1957. *Storytelling for You.* Yellow Springs, Ohio: The Antioch Press.

Dorian, M., and F. Gulland, 1974. *Telling Stories Through Movement.* Belmont, California: Feron Publishers.

Elkind, D., 1978. *The Child's Reality: Three Developmental Themes.* Hillsdale, N.J.: Lawrence Erlbaum Associates.

Ericson, E.H., 1963. *Childhood and Society.* New York: Norton.

Fraiberg, S.H., 1959. *The Magic Years.* New York: Charles Scribner's Sons.

Fromm, E., 1959. *The Forgotten Language: An Introduction to the Understanding of Dreams, Fairy Tales and Myths.* New York: Rinehart and Co.

Gessell, A., F. Ilg, and L.B. Ames, 1943. *Infant and Child in the Culture of Today.* New York: Harper and Row.

Hess, R.D., and D.J. Croft, 1972. *Teachers of Young Children.* New York: Houghton Mifflin Company.

Highberger, R., and C. Schramm, 1976. *Child Development for Day Care Workers.* Boston: Houghton Mifflin Company.

Kincaid, L., 1975. *Time for a Tale, A Collection of Nursery and Fairy Stories.* Cambridge: Brimax Books.

Lines, K., 1961. *The Faber Storybook.* London: Faber and Faber.

Piaget, J., 1962. *Play, Dreams, and Imitation in Childhood.* New York: Norton and Company, Inc.

Ross., R.R., 1972. *Storyteller.* Columbus: Charles E. Merrill Publishing Co.

Scott, L.B., 1959. *Stories That Stick.* Dansville, New York: Instructor Publications.

Schwebel, M., and J. Ralph, 1973. *Piaget in the Classroom.* New York: Basic Books, Inc.

Williams-Ellis, A., 1963. *Fairy Tales from East and West.* London: Blackie.

Williams-Ellis, A., 1963. *Fairy Tales from Everywhere.* London: Blackie.

Notes

Notes

Notes

Notes